Praise

Change Your Questic

"QuestionThinking puts you on the playir ... se truly effective leaders who have the cou... ust what to ask and how. You can't underestimate the power of inquiry ... his book will make a measurable difference in your life—both professionally and personally."
> —Debra Benton, author of *How to Think Like a CEO* and
> *Lions Don't Need to Roar*

"In Congress or the physics lab, I have tried to develop the important skill of asking myself the tough questions, framed in a way that they can be answered constructively. Marilee Adams' enlightening new book teaches, in a clever, readable way, techniques for asking the right questions so we can achieve preferred outcomes in our professions, friendships, and personal lives. I think I can see improvement already."
> —U.S. Congressman Rush Holt

"I read this book cover to cover *twice*. I had valuable insights each time! It helped me change some of the processes by which I attempt to understand and cooperate with nature. I also thought about how useful it would be for politicians and diplomats to use Dr. Adams' questioning methodologies. It could make our world a safer place."
> —David Pensak, Ph.D., Chief Computer Scientist,
> E.I. DuPont de Nemours, Inc.

"Marilee's new book is an amazing conversation. With clarity and accessibility, she models a process whereby we can intentionally change our way of internal inquiry. Imagine being in conscious charge of our own thoughts! A wonderful tool for coaches, helping professionals, and all who desire to transform their inner conversations."
> —Pamela Richarde, M.A. Master Certified Coach

"This is the best book I have ever read on using questions for self-development, career success, and organizational development. It is an invaluable aid to healthy thinking and creative decision-making. This is a splendid achievement."
> —Ronald Gross, author of *Socrates' Way* and
> Chair, University Seminar on Innovation,
> Columbia University

"Great read! If you are going to get to the 'heart of change' you have to ask the right questions. This book hits the bull's eye."
> —Dan S. Cohen, coauthor (with John Kotter) of
> *The Heart of Change*

"A breath of fresh air. Marilee Adams helps open the door to innovation, creativity, and inspiration. This book is a treasure chest."
> —Harrison Owen, author of *The Spirit of Leadership* and
> founder of Open Space Technology

"This book is great. I couldn't put it down! It clearly communicates how the questions we ask ourselves and others determine our results—including in sales. I am strongly recommending this *Change Your Questions, Change Your Life* to everyone who takes my sales courses."

> —Jacques Werth, coauthor of *High Probability Selling*

"This fable is destined to be a classic in the genre of *Who Moved My Cheese?* QuestionThinking will make your life more effective regardless of personal history, personality type, or profession. Buy this book and read it tonight. Your life will never be the same."

> —Stewart Levine, author of *The Book of Agreement* and
> *Getting to Resolution*

"This book is an invitation to success for individuals and organizations. Dr. Marilee Adams has created a surprisingly simple practice to help move *away* from judgments that prevent success and *toward* learning that propels us to our goals. Best of all, the same practices that make a difference for individuals also offer practical guidelines for learning organizations."

> —Victoria J. Marsick, Ph.D., coauthor of
> *Sculpting the Learning Organization* and
> Professor, Teachers College, Columbia University

"This eminently readable tale shows how a business executive matures into a successful inquiring leader. Dr. Marilee Adams' Learner-Judger mindset model gets to the heart of a healing practice for people in all walks of life. This book teaches one to question, listen, and learn; it presents a method that promotes genuine dialogue. It should be a bestseller."

> —Professor Maurice Friedman, Ph.D., author of
> *Martin Buber: The Life of Dialogue*

"Questions, more than answers, have the power to change our lives. Question-Thinking brings you into a world of successful decision-making. This book delivers the goods: transformation, improved judgment, and innovation. Can a book really change your life? The answer is 'Yes!'"

> —Hildy and Stan Richelson, authors of
> *The Money-Making Guide to Bonds*

"The greatest leaders possess a powerful combination of courage, wisdom, and open-mindedness. Marilee shows how these skills are attainable through this wonderful story. She is smarter than anyone I know about asking the questions that really matter."

> —Lillian Brown, author of *Your Public Best* and
> *The Polished Politician,* named "one of the 100 most
> influential PR people of the century" by *PR Week*

change your questions change your life

7 powerful tools for life and work

Marilee G. Adams, Ph.D.

BK

BERRETT–KOEHLER PUBLISHERS, INC.
San Francisco

Berrett-Koehler Publishers, Inc.
235 Montgomery Street, Suite 650
San Francisco, CA 94104-2916
Tel: (415) 288-0260   Fax: (415) 362-2512   www.bkconnection.com

Ordering Information

Quantity sales. Special discounts are available on quantity purchases by corporations, associations, and others. For details, contact the "Special Sales Department" at the Berrett-Koehler address above.

Individual sales. Berrett-Koehler publications are available through most bookstores. They can also be ordered direct from Berrett-Koehler: Tel: (800) 929-2929; Fax: (802) 864-7626; www.bkconnection.com

Orders for college textbook/course adoption use. Please contact Berrett-Koehler: Tel: (800) 929-2929; Fax: (802) 864-7626.

Orders by U.S. trade bookstores and wholesalers. Please contact Publishers Group West, 1700 Fourth Street, Berkeley, CA 94710. Tel: (510) 528-1444; Fax (510) 528-3444.

Berrett-Koehler and the BK logo are registered trademarks of Berrett-Koehler Publishers, Inc.

Printed in the United States of America

Berrett-Koehler books are printed on long-lasting acid-free paper. When it is available, we choose paper that has been manufactured by environmentally responsible processes. These may include using trees grown in sustainable forests, incorporating recycled paper, minimizing chlorine in bleaching, or recycling the energy produced at the paper mill.

Library of Congress Cataloging-in-Publication Data
Adams, Marilee G., 1945–
    Change your questions, change your life : 7 powerful tools for life and work / Marilee G. Adams.
        p. cm.
    Includes bibliographical references.
    ISBN 1-57675-241-0
        1. Change (Psychology).   2. Self-talk.   I. Title.
BF637.C4A33 2004
158.1—dc22   2003063943

FIRST EDITION
09 08 07 06 05 04   10 9 8 7 6 5 4 3 2

Text design by Detta Penna

*For Ed Adams,
my husband and muse.*

Contents

v

Foreword

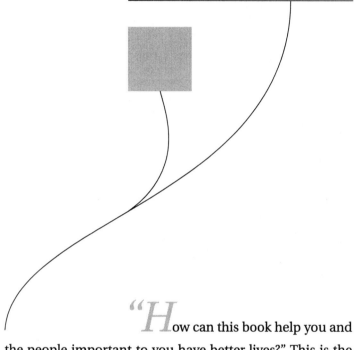

"*H*ow can this book help you and the people important to you have better lives?" This is the key question I urge you to keep in mind as you read this valuable book. The great ideas presented here, in a system of tools Marilee Adams calls QuestionThinking, provide a solid new way of thinking that can make a positive difference in all our lives.

There are many ideas in this book that helped me. You're sure to find some that will help you, too. *Change Your Questions, Change Your Life* provides methods, skills, and tools for easily implementing QuestionThinking both at home and at work. To begin with, Marilee shows how we can become more effective and efficient by focusing on learning rather than judging. As a Buddhist, I know this is key to having a happier, more productive life.

Marilee shows us the power of questions to direct our thinking, and therefore our actions and results. This means that we can intentionally affect the future by designing the most powerful questions for getting us there. That's what great coaching is all about. It's also what great leaders do—they provide us with visions of new futures. Marilee offers question tools for both coaches and leaders to optimize and fulfill their missions.

In my mission as an executive coach, I help successful leaders get better measurable results. This includes teaching a process called feed*forward*. Leaders learn to ask for ideas to improve the future. They refine their ability to listen without judgment and to say "thank you" for suggestions. Marilee would call this "Learner listening." This is invaluable for all coaches, leaders, and managers.

Racecar drivers are taught to "focus on the road—not the wall." As you read this book, focus on the road that represents your highest potential by asking questions that lead to a better future, such as "What are the greatest possibilities I can imagine?"

Change Your Questions, Change Your Life has great wisdom for us all. Take it very seriously. Roll up your sleeves and get to work. The best way to get the most *out* of this book is to practice everything *in* it!

Life is good!

Marshall Goldsmith

Author, *The Leader of the Future* and *Coaching for Leadership*
Named by the American Management Association as one of
50 great thinkers and leaders who have influenced
the field of management over the past 80 years

Acknowledgments

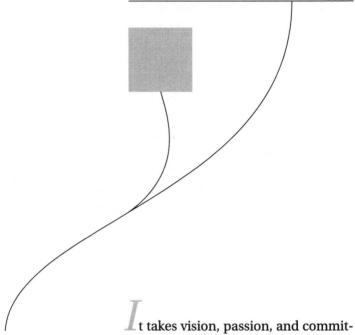

*I*t takes vision, passion, and commitment to bring dreams into reality. It also takes an extraordinary amount of support. My lifelong dream is to share the benefits and skills of QuestionThinking with as many people as possible. Happily, I have the opportunity to express my heartfelt gratitude to those whose support helped me and helped me to fulfill this part of that dream.

Hal Zina Bennett brought an exceptional wealth of wisdom, experience, and generosity to our writing partnership and our friendship. His well-honed skills helped bring the QuestionThinking message to life. For Hal, a superlative wordsmith, my appreciation is beyond words.

Andrea Zintz, my partner at the Center for Inquiring Leadership, has been an inspirational, loving, and stalwart support. It is the gift of a lifetime to have a friend believe in one so fully. Danielle LaPorte Johnson and Michelle Pante helped articulate and anchor the vision and accompanied me expertly and passionately on the journey. Lauren Yeh provided caring and thorough daily support that allowed me to devote myself to this work. Sam Kirschner contributed brilliantly to the proposal that grew into this book. Stewart Levine introduced me to Berrett-Koehler. Diane Chew gifted me with the title.

My husband, Ed Adams, provided loving support in uncountable ways. I feel lucky every day that we share our lives together.

Each of these friends and colleagues also contributed substantially and generously and I am deeply grateful: Rose Adams, Zak Adams, Robert Allen, Kelley Banks, Joan Barth, Frank Basler, Ilene Becker, Larry Becker, Alexandra Zintz Bernstein, David Bernstein, Jessica Zintz Bernstein, Josh Bernstein (Boulder Outdoor Survival School), Pat Brewer, Beth Brody, Rob Burger, Ron Bynum, Dolores Calicchio, Craig Clark, Dan Cohen, Wayne Coleson, David Cooper-rider, Elizabeth Corley, Robin Donovan, Kathleen Epperson, Marilyn Figlar, Vincent Firth, David Fisher,

Ellen Gauthier, LeRoy Goldberg, Veronica Guns, Mark Victor Hansen, Mia Hansen, Kathleen Higgins, Hallock Hoffman, Rebel Holiday, Lynne Hornyak, Susan Horowitz, Harper LaPorte Johnson, Judy Keegan, Roy Plummer, Florence Kaslow, Maggie Larkin, Mark Levy, Sharon Lockhart, Tom Lutes, Nusa Maal, Sean Mason, Hyman Meyers, Harrison Owen, Detta Penna, Laura Pedro, Artie Pine, Brad Pressman, Gerry Pulvermacher, Audrey Reed, Hildy Richelson, Stan Richelson, Lee Salmon, Marge Schiller, Lindsay Simmonds, Melinda Sinclair, Mavis Smith, Mark Steisel, Linda Noble Topf, Sandra Tripp, Susan Walters, and Lou Wolfe.

Berrett-Koehler is a visionary publisher, and I am honored to be one of their authors. I am forever grateful to Steve Piersanti, founder of Berrett-Koehler, who championed my dream of bringing the benefits of Question-Thinking to individuals and organizations. The same enthusiasm and dedication have been consistently demonstrated by the entire Berrett-Koehler team, especially Jenny Hermann, Dianne Platner, Jeevan Sivasubramaniam, and Rick Wilson. I thank you all.

Introduction

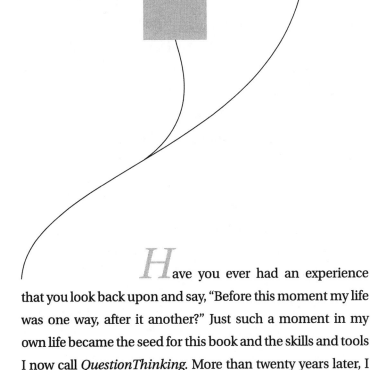

*H*ave you ever had an experience that you look back upon and say, "Before this moment my life was one way, after it another?" Just such a moment in my own life became the seed for this book and the skills and tools I now call *QuestionThinking*. More than twenty years later, I still look back at that time with gratitude. The work it inspired has impacted not only my life but that of many others. Let me share the story of that life-altering moment with you.

I can recall it as if it were yesterday. I was on the phone with my Ph.D. advisor, waiting for feedback on some work I felt great about. Holding my breath, I waited for

Hallock's praise. Instead, I heard him say, "Marilee, this is just not acceptable."

My stomach did a somersault. *Did I hear him right?* In those days, comments that felt critical often left me in tears. For years I had worked to silence my inner critic and become more accepting of myself. Although I'd made some progress, I hadn't seen great evidence that my efforts had been fruitful. But at this moment, something occurred that felt like a miracle.

Instead of the old tearful reaction, I became calm and curious. With ease, I responded to my advisor, "Okay, how do I fix it?"

An observer part of me watched all this and asked incredulously, *Was that me? What had happened? How was I able to switch my mood so easily?* Resolving to figure it out, I also wondered: *Could this seeming miracle be turned into a method to pass along to others?*

I discovered that what had happened was a fundamental change in the kinds of questions I usually asked myself. The old me asked mostly worried questions, such as *Does he like and approve of me?* and *What did I do wrong?* The new me had started operating out of calm, productive questions like *How can I make this work? What can I learn?* and *What's possible?* By changing the kinds of questions I asked, I changed my life.

Until we develop the ability to *cause* the kind of change I experienced, we are at the mercy of other people's opinions and the whims of our own moods. *The ability to intentionally shift our internal questions puts us in charge of our own thoughts.* This book shows you how to do that.

Change Your Questions, Change Your Life is the story of Ben Knight. He finds himself challenged, seemingly beyond his limits, in his new promotion to a highly responsible management position. Convinced he doesn't have what it takes, he drafts his resignation. That's when his CEO steps in and gives him a second chance by introducing him to Joseph Edwards, the inquiring coach. However, Ben's job isn't his only problem. His marriage is also in trouble. In the pages ahead you'll follow Ben through the transformations he makes, both at work and at home.

Ben's story is just one of many, drawn from personal accounts women and men have shared with me over the years. Even as I write these words, I'm reminded of a woman named Susan who attended one of my early workshops. Susan's story stands out because she experienced a dramatic change, similar to what I had with my professor. I want to tell you about her to give you a glimpse of what's ahead for you in these pages.

Toward the end of that workshop, I asked if anyone had questions. Susan raised her hand somewhat tentatively. When I called on her, she told us about a problem she was having at work. She blurted out, "I hate my boss!" She tearfully told us how working for Phillip, the principal of the school where she taught, had become intolerable.

Although she loved teaching, she believed she had to quit her job.

Just moments before, we'd been discussing the hidden power of the questions we ask ourselves. These internal questions—*Self-Q's*—can either hurt us or help us, even when we don't know they're there. It turned out that Susan was asking the hurting kind. I call them *troublemaker questions*.

"It all just seems so hopeless and complicated," she sighed, shaking her head in despair.

I reassured her, "Actually, this method is far easier than it seems. It's simply a two-step change process: First, identify the Self-Q's you've been asking. Second, change them if you think different questions might produce better results."

In just a few minutes we figured out Susan's troublemaker questions. Both were about her boss: *What's he going to do wrong this time?* and *How's he going to make me look bad?*

It was obvious that Susan's boss didn't have a chance with her, given those negative Self-Q's. The two questions set up an ambush he just couldn't escape. There was simply no way he could do anything right in her eyes.

Once she had identified her troublemaker questions, we were ready for step two of the process. Now we needed a helping question, the kind that would make the difference Susan wanted so much. She needed a question to program her for success rather than failure. The new one I suggested was: *What can I do to make my boss look good?* I thought she was going to argue with me. But she promised to give it a try.

A few months later, by sheer coincidence, I ran into Susan and her husband, Carl, at the supermarket. I reintroduced myself and told her I was curious about how things had gone for her since the workshop.

"Would you like to hear a miracle?" she responded with a big smile. Three remarkable improvements had occurred since our interaction. Susan had received a raise. She had been promoted. And, amazingly, she was working on a committee with Phillip, the boss she'd once hated. She laughed as she recalled how she'd previously avoided even being in the same room with him.

At this point, Carl put his arm around Susan and commented, "Susan's breakthrough with her boss brought peace to our home. Before your workshop, she used to complain about that guy every night. Now she hardly ever talks about him. Life got a lot better for her at work. And I'm happier because things are much better between us!"

Susan and Carl mentioned several times how miraculous this all seemed. But I knew better. It wasn't a miracle at all. It was the *method* I developed after that moment with my professor, when my new questions dramatically changed my view of the world and what was possible for me.

The changes in many people like Susan, along with similar experiences of my own, convinced me to write this book. I wanted to share the benefits of QuestionThinking with as many people as possible. I know these skills really work because I've applied them to every part of my life. Everything has changed for the better, from my sense of confidence to my career, marriage, health, weight, and finances.

I first wrote about these tools in a professional text titled, *The Art of the Question: A Guide to Short-Term Question-Centered Therapy.* As a result of that book, and workshops I've presented on this process, I often receive feedback from people on how they've used QuestionThinking to be more successful in virtually every area of their lives, especially in their relationships and careers.

The most common theme of all this feedback is people's relief at having found a "how-to" that *actually works—* one that puts them in charge of their own thinking and therefore their own results. As one workshop participant recently told me, "This work has changed my whole philosophy of life, and the best thing is that it's so *practical.* It shows me exactly how to make the changes I want."

I developed the QuestionThinking system during my early career as a therapist. These tools are equally powerful in organizational consulting and executive coaching. I've been fortunate to serve diverse clients, from the most elite Fortune 100 companies to nonprofit organizations, and the Federal government, including the military. These clients have proven, time and time again, that QuestionThinking is invaluable in leadership development, team effectiveness, productivity, and innovation.

The ability to think productively rather than reactively lies at the heart of QuestionThinking. It is the key to building high emotional intelligence and making wise choices wherever we are. In this way QT methods also help empower successful learning organizations.

As you read Ben Knight's story and follow his progress, you'll get a clear picture of how the Question-Thinking system works. Following Ben's story is a workbook that shows you how to use the same QuestionThinking tools and practices that led him to such remarkable results. While the seven tools are woven together throughout the story, in the workbook you'll find each one described separately, with clear, step-by-step instructions. Put these tools to work for yourself. I believe you'll be happy with your results.

Over the years of teaching QuestionThinking, one thing has become abundantly clear to me: A world of questions is a world of possibility. Questions open our minds, connect us to each other, and shake outmoded paradigms. I have a vision of a workforce and a society—of individuals, families, institutions, and communities—that are vibrant with the spirit of inquiry. Our orientation would shift from one of answers and opinions to one of questions and curiosity. We would see quick judgments, fixed perspectives, and old opinions give way to exploration, discovery, innovation, and cooperation.

What makes this kind of change so practical is that it begins with each one of us, right here, right now. We have only to ask the right questions to begin.

Moment of Truth

A rosewood paperweight on my desk bears a sterling silver plaque declaring: *Great results begin with great questions.* It was a gift from a very special person in my life—Joseph S. Edwards—who introduced me to QuestionThinking, or QT, as he called the skills he taught me. QT opened up a part of my mind that otherwise I might never have discovered. Like everyone else, I believed the way to fix a problem was to go on a hunt for answers. Instead, Joseph showed me that the best way to solve a problem is to first come up with better questions. The skills he taught me rescued my career and saved my marriage as well. Both were definitely in trouble at the time.

It all started when I was invited to take a management position at QTec, Inc. Just before I came aboard, Wall Street naysayers predicted the company would fold before the year was out. You might wonder why I took a position on a sinking ship. It wasn't an easy decision. Alexa Harte had recently been appointed CEO at QTec, and Alexa and I had worked together for years at AZ Corp. She invited me to join QTec, saying there were no guarantees but she believed the company could be turned around. It was a great promotion, and there were excellent stock options. If everything worked out, the risk would pay off in aces. If not . . . well, I tried not to think about that.

At first I was riding high, convinced I had the job wired. I had the answers and I was bound for success. Then things unraveled pretty fast. Suddenly it was as if a glaring spotlight had been focused on my shortcomings. The people on my team were going off in all directions. It was obvious they were avoiding me. I blamed my problems on Charles, a co-worker whom I saw as blocking my efforts to pull the team together. Things went from bad to worse when our production schedule fell apart. This was a big deal because the future of the company largely depended on getting our product to market ahead of the competition. I was in more trouble than I cared to admit.

Things weren't much better at home. Grace, my wife

of eight months, knew something was wrong. I'd tried to keep the truth from her, believing it was best to keep work and home separate. Grace didn't buy that. She insisted being married meant sharing both our challenges and our victories. She always wanted me to tell her what was going on at work. I told her she was asking too many questions and she should keep her nose out of my business. She was hurt, I was miserable, and I hadn't the vaguest idea what to do about it.

I didn't want her knowing how much difficulty I was having. I'd always taken great pride in solving problems that baffled everyone else. With any luck the right answers would turn up before Grace, Alexa, and my employees found out the job was way over my head. Meanwhile I kept to myself and did my best just to get through each day.

I'll never forget the dark turning point. Grace and I had an argument in the morning and there was a major crisis at work. Later that afternoon I called her office to say I'd be putting in an all-nighter to finish an important report. I spent the next fifteen hours alone in my office, still looking for answers, and reliving two of the most disastrous weeks of my life. The writing was on the wall. It was time to admit defeat. Just after six that morning I went out for coffee and then began drafting my resignation. I finished three hours later, called Alexa, and made arrangements to see her immediately.

The walk to Alexa's suite was less than a hundred

yards. That morning it felt like a hundred miles. When I got to the big double doors of her office, I stopped and took a deep breath to regain my composure. I stood there for some long moments, working up the nerve to knock. Just as I was raising my hand, I heard a voice behind me.

"Ben Knight, you're here. Good, good!"

It was Alexa. There was no mistaking that voice, always cheerful, exuding a sense of optimism even when things were going badly. An attractive, athletic-looking woman in her early fifties, she radiated confidence. I told Grace I'd never met anyone quite like Alexa. She approached her responsibilities at QTec with boundless enthusiasm. It wasn't that she didn't take her job seriously. She did take it seriously, but she did it with such pleasure and self-assurance that she made it look easy.

At that moment, her mere presence made me acutely aware of my own deficiencies. I felt numb, barely mumbling a subdued good morning as she touched my shoulder and ushered me into her office.

The room was expansive, the size of a large living room in the best executive home. I crossed deep green carpeting, soft underfoot, and walked over to the large bay window where the meeting area was set up. There, two overstuffed sofas faced one another across a large walnut coffee table.

"Sit!" Alexa said, gesturing in a welcoming way to one of the couches. "Betty said your lights were on when she left her office at seven-thirty last night, and you were here when she came in at eight."

She sat down across from me on the other couch.

"I presume that's for me?" Alexa asked, pointing to the green folder containing my resignation that I'd placed on the coffee table.

I nodded, waiting for her to pick it up. Instead, she leaned back, looking as if she had all the time in the world.

"Tell me what's going on with you," she said.

I pointed to the green folder. "It's my resignation. I'm sorry, Alexa."

The next sound I heard stopped me cold. It was not a gasp, not a word of reproach, but laughter! It was not mean laughter, either. What had I missed? I didn't understand. How could Alexa still sound sympathetic in the face of all I'd screwed up?

"Ben," she said, "you're not going to quit on me." She slid the folder in my direction. "Take this back. I know more about your situation than you realize. I want you to give me six more weeks. But in this time, you have to commit to making changes."

"Are you sure of this?" I asked, dumbfounded.

"Let me answer you this way," she continued. "Long ago, I was in a situation similar to yours. I had to face facts. If I wanted to be successful I'd have to make some fundamental changes. I was pretty desperate. A man by the name of Joseph sat me down and asked some straightforward questions, simple ones on the surface. But those questions opened doors I never even knew existed. He asked, 'Are you willing to take responsibility for your mistakes—and for the attitudes and actions that led to them?' Then he said, 'Are you willing—however begrudgingly—to forgive yourself, and even laugh at yourself?' And finally, 'Will you look for value in your experiences, especially the most difficult ones?' Bottom line, 'Are you willing to learn from what happened and make changes accordingly?'"

She went on to tell me how Joseph's work changed not only her life but her husband's as well. "Stan has tripled his income in the past few years. He attributes the success he and his company enjoy today to what Joseph taught him. Joseph would tell you all about it. He loves to tell stories, especially ones about how people's lives were changed by changing their questions."

I must have looked perplexed because she added, "Don't worry about what I mean by questions that change people's lives. You'll learn about that soon enough." She paused. Then, in carefully measured words, she said, "I want you to work with my friend Joseph, starting immediately. I'm sure he'll want to meet with you a number of times over the next six weeks. Work out the schedule with him. This is top priority now."

"What is he, a psychotherapist?" The idea of seeing a shrink made me nervous.

Alexa smiled. "No, he's an executive coach. I call him an *inquiring coach.*"

Inquiring coach! If I knew anything at all, it was that I needed answers, not more questions. What good could more questions possibly be to me?

As I left, Alexa jotted something down and sealed it in an envelope. "Inside this envelope is a prediction I've made," she said mysteriously, handing it to me. "Put it in that green folder of yours and don't open it until you've completed your work with Joseph." Then she gave me his business card. I turned it over. There was a big question mark on the other side. It really irritated me. The idea that I'd be spending valuable time with a man whose logo was a question mark went against everything I believed.

Back in my own office, I collapsed in the chair behind my desk. My eyes fell on a small gilded frame on the wall. It held a saying, just two words long: *Question every-thing!* It was a quote attributed to Albert Einstein. Many rooms at QTec contained a framed placard exactly like this one. As much as I respected and appreciated Alexa's leader-ship, this had always been a point of contention for me. Leaders should have answers, not questions.

I was still holding Joseph's card with the question mark on the back. What had I gotten myself into? Only time would tell. I was grateful that I could put off my decision to resign. That was at least on hold. My attention then shifted to Grace. How was I ever going to smooth things over with her? At least Alexa hadn't asked about Grace and me. I think that would have been the last straw. I knew Alexa was fond of my wife—she'd even come to our wedding. She wouldn't have been happy to find out we were having trouble.

I sat there for a long time just staring at Joseph's card. The fact that Alexa had refused to accept my resignation gave me a little hope. I was encouraged that she thought enough of me to refer me to her own mentor, this inquiring coach guy. The jury was still out on whether her trust was deserved, but I had nothing to lose by keeping an appointment with Joseph. Besides, even though I was skeptical, I was also curious about him. If he'd helped Alexa and Stan, maybe he had answers that would help me, too.

Question everything!

A Challenge Accepted

2

*M*y appointment with Joseph S. Edwards was at ten the next morning. I didn't tell Grace about this meeting nor about my conversation with Alexa. And I certainly didn't tell her about writing my resignation. Admitting I was in trouble had never come easy for me. Until I found the right answers and solutions, I was determined to tough it out and keep my problems to myself.

I wasn't so good at hiding my problems from Grace, however. Nearly every night she asked more questions that, frankly, I was resenting. I reacted by stonewalling her and telling her to be patient.

I should have realized she knew something more than the usual job stress was bothering me. She brought things to a head the morning of my meeting with Joseph. We were on our way to the airport where she was catching a plane for a meeting in another city. As we pulled into the terminal, she told me, "I've been feeling like a widow lately. You've been so distant and moody. Ben, if you want a real partnership with me, you're going to have to make some changes."

God knows I love Grace, but I wasn't in the best of moods.

"I don't need this right now," I told her, more harshly than I intended.

Grace looked stunned. I got out of the car and went around to open the door for her. I knew it wasn't right leaving her like that, but I was feeling pushed. Besides, I knew I'd be late for my appointment with Joseph if I got involved in a long discussion. Our little problem would have to wait. Grace forced a smile, told me she'd be back that night, but not to worry about picking her up. She'd get the express shuttle home. She turned and quickly disappeared into the crowd.

I was angry. *Why did she have to choose this particular morning to pick a fight?* I hit the accelerator and pulled out into traffic. Horns blasted. I slammed on my brakes as some maniac raced by, barely missing me. I was fuming. Between that near collision, the conflict with Grace, and having to attend a meeting I dreaded, my morning was off to a very bad start.

Joseph's office was in the Pearl Building downtown, a fourteen-story edifice constructed in the 1930s and recently restored. Old Town, as we called the area, was a bustling shopping center with coffee shops, boutiques, and upscale restaurants. Grace and I often had dinner there, at a small place called the Metropol. She and I spent many happy hours together, browsing through bookstores and art galleries. Until Grace came into my life, I'd never spent my time that way. Now I loved it. Passing our familiar haunts that morning, I worried about what the future held for us.

I pushed open the polished brass-framed doors at the Pearl Building, crossed the marble floors, and caught an elevator to Joseph's penthouse office. I stepped into a large foyer that looked like someone's private residence. Several large ficus trees, each almost ten feet tall, reached up toward a large skylight.

Beyond this private anteroom, a double set of doors was opened invitingly. A long hallway stretched beyond them. The walls inside were polished mahogany, on which hung some kind of artwork. I remember thinking that Grace should see this. Being in the business of art, she would appreciate it.

"You must be Ben Knight!" Joseph Edwards strode rapidly toward me, greeting me enthusiastically. I judged him to be in his early 60s, though he moved like an agile sprinter a quarter that age. He was dressed casually, wearing an outrageous sweater knit with a myriad of brightly colored striped patterns.

Joseph's smooth-shaven face glowed with good humor. His brown eyes sparkled with excitement, almost childlike. Atop his head, a wild array of woolly white curls reminded me of photos I'd seen of Albert Einstein in his later years.

Joseph's warm welcome dissolved some of my reservations about spending time with him. He led me down the hallway to his office, explaining as we went that the walls displayed "some artifacts I call my *QuestionThinking Hall of Fame.*" The hangings I had glimpsed were not artwork, as I'd originally thought, but framed magazine articles and letters. We turned left into a large room bathed in the morning sunlight.

The room contained comfortable seating, a fireplace with a marble hearth, and a walnut conference table with matching chairs. One wall displayed university certificates and at least two dozen autographed photos, many with their subjects shaking hands with Joseph. I recognized in the pictures faces I'd seen in the news over the years. Alexa hadn't quite prepared me for this. Joseph was obviously very well connected in the business world and beyond.

I also saw covers of three different books displayed in elegant frames. They were all written by Joseph. Each had the word *QuestionThinking* in the title. One in particular caught my eye because it was co-authored with a Sarah Edwards. His wife perhaps? The title was *The Inquiring Marriage.*

I was impressed but also intimidated. We entered a less formal room, where I felt slightly more at ease. Colorful Persian rugs graced the floor, while huge windows on three sides afforded a spectacular view of the city. In the distance, wispy clouds were lifting from the forest. The views seemed to stretch on forever.

I eased myself into a large leather armchair while Joseph took his place near me in a matching one. He dangled a pair of rimless reading glasses from his left hand.

After some brief get-acquainted conversation, he asked, "Tell me, what do you suppose is your greatest asset?"

"I'm the *Answer Man,* the *Go-To* guy," I told him with pride. "I've built my whole career around being the person people go to for answers. The bottom line for me is answers. That's what business is all about."

"True. But how can you get the best answers without the best questions?" Joseph paused, placing his glasses on his nose and peering over the top of them at me: "Is there a single question you would say characterizes the way you operate?"

"Sure," I said. "Get the right answers and be ready to back them up, that's my motto."

Joseph asked me to restate that as a question, one I

would ask myself. I couldn't see the point, but I did as he asked, "I guess it would be, 'How can I prove I'm right?'"

"That's great," Joseph said. "Then we've probably got your problem nailed already."

"My problem?"

"Being the Answer Man. Proving you're right," Joseph said. "I've got to tell you, Ben, we're getting down to business faster than I expected."

I wasn't sure if I'd heard him correctly. *Was he kidding? No, he was dead serious.* "I beg your pardon?"

"Finding proof that our answers are correct can be important," he said. "But would you allow that there are times when too much of a good thing can get you in trouble? For example, how do you think your having to be right goes over with your team?"

"I'm not sure what you mean," I said. For the life of me, I was telling the truth. That was the day I began to realize how little I understood about my impact on other people. I'm embarrassed to say, I'd never given it a lot of thought.

"Let me ask you another question," Joseph said. "How does proving you're right go over with your wife?"

That one hit home. Grace had told me how my habit of insisting on being right often frustrated her.

"Everyone's looking for answers," I finally replied in my own defense.

Joseph nodded thoughtfully, pushed his glasses up

Change Your Questions, Change Your Life

on his nose, then said, "Of course, but let's look a little deeper into what questions really do. Right now you probably think about them the same as most people—that they're just sort of there. Certainly we recognize that questions are a vital part of communication. But the role they play in thinking is not always obvious, and that's where QuestionThinking methods come in.

"If you're willing to grab onto the real power of questions, they can change your whole life. It all comes down to increasing the quantity and quality of the questions we ask ourselves and each other."

I must have looked puzzled because Joseph paused and said, "You've never heard the term QuestionThinking before, have you?"

I shook my head, no.

"QuestionThinking is a system of tools using questions to expand how you approach virtually any situation. These tools give you the power to refine your questions for vastly better results in anything you do. The system can literally put action into your thinking—action that's both focused and effective. It's a great way to create a foundation for making wiser choices."

"Go on," I said, skeptically.

"Most of the time we're barely conscious of asking questions. But they're part of our thought process nearly every moment of our lives. Thinking actually occurs as a question and answer process. Here's an example. When you

A Challenge Accepted

got dressed this morning, I'll bet you went to your closet, or dresser—or maybe even the floor—and asked yourself questions that might have included some of these: *Where am I going? What's the weather? What's comfortable?* Or even, *What's clean?* You answered your questions by *doing* something. You selected some clothing and put it on. You are, in effect, wearing your answer."

"I guess I can't argue with that. As you say, though, if I did ask those questions, I hardly noticed at the time. Actually, my biggest question was whether Grace picked up my suit at the cleaners, like she promised."

We both laughed.

> *QuestionThinking is a system of tools for transforming thinking, action, and results through skillful question asking—questions we ask ourselves as well as those we ask others.*

I could tell Joseph was getting on a roll. I decided to just sit back and hear him out.

"When we get stuck, it's natural to look for answers and solutions. But in so doing we can unwittingly create blocks instead of openings. We first need to change our questions; otherwise we just keep recycling the same old, unhelpful answers.

"New questions can totally shift our perspectives, moving us into fresh ways of looking at and solving problems. Questions have even changed the course of history. Let me give you a dramatic example. Think about this—nomadic societies were driven by the implicit question, 'How do we get ourselves to water?'"

I nodded. "Which is what kept them nomadic. . . ."

"Yet look what happened when the question changed to, 'How do we get water to come to us?' That new question initiated one of humanity's most significant paradigm shifts. It ushered in agriculture and eventually the invention of cities."

"I guess I can see how questions apply to getting dressed and to nomads looking for water. But how does this apply to business? And more to the point, how can it help me with my problems at work?"

"First of all, let me assure you that it *can* help in your situation at work! As for its application in business, my *QuestionThinking Hall of Fame* is filled with people just like you, who changed their lives by learning to ask new questions.

"Remember, the point is that questions drive results. They virtually program how we behave and what kinds of outcomes are possible. Consider three companies, each one driven by one of the following questions: *What's the* best way to satisfy shareholders? What's the best way to satisfy customers? What's the best way to satisfy employees?* Each question focuses on a different aspect of doing business. Each will have a different influence on priorities, everyday behavior, and strategies for achieving goals. Imagine the results of a company responding to all three of these questions! Remember, the results you get will be driven by the questions you ask."

"Your ideas are interesting," I hedged. "But maybe you're forgetting, I'm an Answer Man. I've literally built my reputation on having answers . . . not questions."

"Fortunately," Joseph continued, "the route from being an Answer Man to becoming a Question Man is much shorter than you might think."

What was he suggesting? Giving up my Answer Man role was the furthest thing from my mind. I wasn't about to give up something that had worked so well for me for so long. One thing I was pretty certain of—if we'd stuck only with questions, we'd still be scratching our heads and hunting for our suppers with pointed sticks.

Joseph removed his glasses and proceeded to swing them back and forth, as if contemplating carefully what he was going to say next. He took a breath, then spoke in a slow, even voice.

"Ben, you've got to face facts here—you're in trouble. One of your greatest assets—being an Answer Man—has turned into a liability. That's the bottom line."

As Joseph spoke, I imagined Grace sitting here in Joseph's office with me. Truly, she would applaud what he was saying. A big knot tightened in my belly.

"Ben, let's be straight with each other. If your being the Answer Man was still working so well, you wouldn't have spent the night in your office writing your resignation. Alexa told me you did that. I know where you were coming from. I've had my own share of all-night debates with the walls of my office.

"This is where I think I can help you," he continued. "Alexa believes you've got great potential, and she's obviously invested a lot in you. But she also thinks that without some big changes you won't make it at QTec. She knows you pretty well, Ben. She shared her concerns with me about bringing you into the company. If I'm not mistaken, she also told you what she was worried about. Alexa is not exactly a shrinking violet."

We both laughed at that comment, and I was grateful for a moment of levity. Alexa was about the most forthright human being I'd ever met. She never beat around the bush.

With considerable embarrassment, I remembered her words the day she hired me: "Ben, I'm bringing you in because you're absolutely the best in your field. I'm completely confident about your technical acumen, which we need for the new markets we plan to open up. What I'm not so comfortable with is your management style. I'm gambling on you, and I plan on winning this bet."

The truth is, I had brushed off Alexa's warning. Instead, I had immediately called Grace to tell her about my great coup. If I had heard Alexa's warning at all, it was filtered through the plans I was making for a victory celebration that evening.

"As an Answer Man," Joseph continued, "your dogged determination to find the right answers led you to some brilliant breakthroughs. However, the line between having the right answers and being perceived as a know-it-all is a thin one, indeed. You could even come off as arrogant. My guess is that with the added pressure and responsibility of your new position, that know-it-all style got exaggerated. Once you get labeled, you're in trouble. When others start seeing you that way, can you really expect them to like you? It's not exactly an ideal leadership profile."

"Who's running a popularity contest here?" I countered. In my mind, a good leader had one responsibility—to get the job done and see that others followed through on their assignments. Nobody on my team was producing.

"Whenever you're interacting with other people," Joseph said, "you want them to take initiative, to ask their own questions, and come up with answers that maybe you hadn't thought of yourself. Your accomplishments come from the total efforts of the people you're working with, not just from your own solitary work. If you really are coming off as a know-it-all, you make it virtually impossible for any one else to even make a suggestion. This position can be a disaster for leaders. You leave no room to understand where other people are coming from or for them to make a contribution."

Joseph was on target about some things, but I was still having real trouble with his emphasis on questions. Everyone has questions, that's a no-brainer. But it's the guy with answers who makes things happen.

"You've hit a wall, Ben. If you're going to climb over it," Joseph said, "you've got to start asking more questions. You've got to do a lot more asking than telling. The most effective communication is about 20 percent telling and 80 percent asking. You'd be amazed at how many things in your life would improve just by paying attention to that one principle. Most of us have it turned around—80 percent telling and 20 percent asking."

That last comment really got to me. *Telling* had been my *modus operandi* for as long as I could remember. On the other hand, if my old assumptions were still working so well, what was I doing in Joseph's office? Should I be questioning my own assumption about the power of answers? I was beginning to suspect I might miss something important if I didn't listen to Joseph's ideas. The notion that Grace might agree with him was also playing at the back of my mind. Was I doing too much telling and not enough asking with her? I suspect I already knew the answer to that question.

"Judging by the look on your face, I'm guessing you're a little unsettled right now," Joseph said. "But I assure you that once you understand how to use the Question-

A Challenge Accepted

Thinking system, all the pieces will fall into place. You have no idea what a powerful difference this can make for your career." Then he gave me an enigmatic smile and added, "To say nothing of what it can do for your personal relationships."

QuestionThinking! This was going to be tough. Even Joseph's terms for his theories got to me. Wasn't it bad enough that he wanted me to ask myself and other people more questions? No matter. I realized it was time to bite the bullet. I had to try and take in what he had to offer. What choice did I have? I was desperate.

"This system of new tools and processes will make you more efficient, productive, and successful," Joseph continued. "In the end, I believe you'll be able to make a quantum leap out of your present quandary. Despite your doubts, I'm with Alexa on this one. I'm betting on your success."

At this point Joseph declared an intermission, as he jokingly called it.

I made a quick call back to my office. There was nothing that couldn't wait. I was glad for that because I was in no mood to deal with anything else. I guess I was pretty shaken up. Minutes later, in the restroom, I caught my reflection in the mirror. Recently, the face staring back at me had been that of a stranger, filled with tension and anger. Was this the face that Grace had been looking at for the past few months? Truth be told, I wasn't sure I'd want to hang around that guy myself. Could I really change, as Alexa and Joseph seemed to believe? I wasn't so sure.

Discovering Learner and Judger Questions

3

*B*ack in Joseph's office, I was feeling calmer and a bit more open. Besides, I didn't want anyone accusing me of being arrogant or narrow-minded. Joseph immediately turned my attention to a large mural on the wall of the main office and said, "This is what I call the Choice Map."

"Notice the guy standing at the crossroads between the two paths," Joseph continued. "He represents you and

© 2004 Marilee G. Adams, Ph.D. www.InstituteforInquiringLeadership.com
Adapted from *The Art of the Question*. Copyright © 1998 Marilee C. Goldberg, Ph.D.
This material is used by permission of John Wiley & Sons, Inc.

me—every one of us. In every instant of our lives we're faced with choosing between the two paths illustrated by the map—the Learner path and the Judger path. The smaller figures show what questions that guy asks on each path and what happens, depending on which path he takes."

From his chair Joseph directed a laser pointer at the map, swinging it back and forth between two little signs, one said, "Choose," the other said, "React."

I followed Joseph's laser pointer to the upper path, where figures were happily jogging along. This was the Learner path, with the sign indicating you got to it by *choosing*. It looked pretty inviting to me.

The other path, the Judger path, looked downright bleak. It had to do with *reacting* rather than choosing. No happy joggers here. These figures looked troubled as they headed down toward a billboard labeled *Judger.* A smaller sign warned: *Judger Pit.* This warning had obviously come too late for one poor fellow who was sinking in the mud. I chuckled, but my amusement ended abruptly when some unpleasant thoughts raced through my mind: *Was Joseph sending me a covert message? Did he think I was sinking in the mud like that poor guy? Did he think I was a Judger and a loser?*

"What are you thinking?" Joseph asked.

I was too nonplussed to bother trying to cover it up. "Are you implying I'm a Judger?" I looked past him, pretending to study the map. "Or that I'm a loser?"

Change Your Questions, Change Your Life

Joseph answered quickly." You wouldn't be in this office if anybody believed you were a loser. As for your concern about being a Judger, let me answer you this way: Every single one of us has Judger moments, including me. It's a natural part of being human."

"That makes me feel a little better," I ventured, though still ill at ease.

"Let's be clear about this," Joseph continued. "The Choice Map is not about classifying people or putting them in boxes. It's a powerful tool for charting more effective paths through our lives. Its message is so universal that I had this mural painted on my wall. Nobody who visits my office escapes the Choice Map." He spread out his arms expansively. "How could they miss?"

We both laughed and I relaxed a little.

"At nearly every instant of our lives, we're faced with choices," Joseph continued. "Whether we recognize it or not, we're also always choosing between Judger and Learner mindsets. With Judger mindset we eventually end up stuck in the mud. With Learner we discover new paths and possibilities.

"Most of the time, we're shifting back and forth between Learner and Judger paths, barely aware we have any control over which one we've chosen. But we do have choice in every moment. Real choice begins when we can observe our own thinking. After all, if we can't manage our own thinking, how can we really manage anything else?

Discovering Learner and Judger Questions

"Whichever path we choose starts with questions. The Choice Map literally guides us to ask more productive questions and make wiser choices. Let me make this promise—you can use the Choice Map to help understand, improve, and change virtually any situation.

"How about if we put it to the test right now? We have a tailor-made issue to work with, too, if you're willing to consider what happened when you asked if I thought you were a loser and a Judger. Are you game?"

I nodded uneasily.

"Place yourself at the crossroads," Joseph said, flashing his laser pointer around the figure standing between the Learner and Judger paths. "Something just happened to that guy. Notice the words *Thoughts, Feelings, Circumstances* circling around his head.

"Those words represent anything that impacts us at any moment. Some things that happen to us are unpleasant: You get an unexpected bill or a phone call with terrible news. Maybe someone tells you that a truck just backed into your new car. Stuff like that happens to us all the time, wouldn't you agree?"

I rolled my eyes and thought, *he doesn't know the half of it!*

"But joyous events impact us, too," Joseph continued. "You click on the TV and the reporter announces that your favorite team had an unexpected win. Your boss surprises you with a fabulous job offer, or maybe your spouse sends flowers with a romantic note. You can never tell what life will throw at you."

"I could stand to get more of the good stuff!" I said. "But what's the point here?"

"It comes down to this," Joseph said. "Although we can't always choose what happens to us, we *can* choose what we do with what happens."

"I like that," I said, thinking he should have that statement on the back of his business card instead of that big question mark.

Joseph continued. "Case in point, let's examine the exact moment when I first showed you the Choice Map and you worried I might think you were a loser. What happened in that instant? Your Self-Q's—the questions you asked yourself—put you on the Judger Path, didn't they?"

Damn! He hit the target dead center. It was true. A subtle shock had run through my body, followed by what he called Self-Q's: *Does he think I'm a loser? Does he think I'm sinking in the mud? Does he think I'm hopeless?* All this had taken place in an instant and I hadn't even noticed. But there was no denying that something had hit me and I hated how it felt. Those negative Self-Q's came in under my radar. They slipped past me and affected me even though I didn't notice them at the time.

"In those first instants," Joseph said, "you actually made a choice."

"Yeah, I admit it. I screwed up," I said.

"Whoa!" Joseph exclaimed, holding up his hand. "There's no good or bad, no right or wrong here. There's just what happens and what you do with what happens."

"I guess that's where choice comes in," I said, reflecting on his words.

"That's the essence of QuestionThinking," Joseph said. "Change your questions, change your thinking. The Choice Map lets you step into the position of a neutral and open-minded observer, then notice your moods, thoughts, and behaviors. It's a wonderful way to check out the questions that precipitated them. If only for a moment, you become a spectator watching a movie of your life. This sets the stage for change. It's very different from being so immersed in the situation that you're powerless to make an objective choice."

"I might have experienced this observer situation once or twice," I said. "I'm remembering times when I've caught myself calling somebody by the wrong name. I guess it was the observer part of me that noticed my mistake. You mean there's something useful about that?"

"Very much so. That same observer capacity gives us a chance to reflect and focus on the bigger picture. Without that, you're on automatic pilot, just going along with the program and reacting thoughtlessly. What I'm talking about is developing ways to make intentional, conscious choices rather than just being controlled by events around us. These are essential leadership qualities. Are you with me?"

"I think so," I said.

"A moment ago, when you focused on the Judger Pit, you weren't exactly in observer mode, were you?"

Joseph was right. If I'd been a neutral observer, I wouldn't have reacted as strongly as I did. He had said nothing to even remotely imply I was a Judger or a loser. That judgmental opinion had come from only one person—me. I had gotten in the Judger Pit all by myself!

"From the look on your face," Joseph said, "you've just recognized your own Judger, maybe for the first time. Bravo! You'll understand why I congratulated you later. First I want to tell you a story about something that happened to me just last month."

I shrugged. "Why not?"

"I was in a session with the superintendent of a large construction company," Joseph began. "I spent a long twenty minutes listening to him put down everyone he worked with. According to him, the world is filled with idiots. I was getting pretty fed up with all his judgmental chatter. I felt like kicking him out of my office! Do you get the picture?"

"You were both speeding down the Judger path," I interjected, feeling like a good student.

"Exactly," Joseph admitted. "The questions running through my mind were, *What did I do to deserve this guy? Who does he think he is, judging everyone around him?*"

"All your questions were Judger questions."

"Yes! When I realized what I was doing, I almost

laughed out loud. Here I was judging this man for judging other people. I was in Judger mode as much as he was!"

Joseph obviously enjoyed telling this story on himself. "By working with the Choice Map you get pretty good at catching yourself in Judger. It's a great way to strengthen your observer self. First, you just notice that something's not quite right. Maybe you feel tense, or upset, or just plain blocked. Second, you wake up enough to ask yourself, *Am I in Judger?* If the answer is yes, then you ask, *Is this where I want to be?* In my case, it wasn't. I realized that if I was in Judger, I really couldn't help this guy, and that's what I was being paid to do. It was a good reminder—*nobody can help anyone from a Judger place.*"

"Seems like a good time to cut your losses and back out," I offered.

"Not at all," Joseph replied. "This was the time to watch the movie, to step into my observer self. From there, I could literally switch my thinking from Judger to Learner. In fact, there's a specific kind of question that helps us do that—and appropriately I call it a *Switching question.* The one that worked for me that day was, 'How else can I think about him?'

"Having done that, I was able to identify the Judger question I'd unconsciously been asking myself about the superintendent—*What's wrong with this guy?* Then I had the freedom to choose a very different question: *What does he need?* That was my new Learner question. Instead of labeling him and writing him off, which is what we tend to do in Judger, this new question got me curious about him. You'd be surprised how the Choice Map helps you in situations like this, to see more options and choose more wisely, even under pressure."

I gave this some serious thought. "It seems to me that lots of people go into Judger whenever there's any kind of conflict," I said. "I mean, both people are probably in Judger at the same time. Right? That's pretty normal, isn't it?" I was thinking about that awful moment with Grace at the airport that morning. I wasn't sure about where Grace was, but I couldn't hide from myself the fact that I was in Judger.

"It is," Joseph said. "With both people in Judger, everything comes to a screeching halt. But here's a million dollar tip for you: *When two people are in Judger, the one who wakes up first has an advantage.* That person can choose to go into Learner, be in the driver's seat, and turn the situation around for both of them."

Something clicked for me. I'd noticed after some disagreements with Grace, she could switch from stubbornness to open-mindedness, often very quickly. Her ability to switch always lightened things up between us. I wondered if she did this naturally or if she had some inner trick. She once told me all she did was remember the bigger picture—our relationship was more important than proving she was right. Something else happened, too. When Grace switched like that, I often got calmer. If Joseph's techniques could teach me how to do this on purpose, I'd be way ahead of the game with my office nemesis, Charles.

"By switching my own questions," Joseph continued, "I began to open up to my client, the superintendent. I asked myself, *What's really going on with him? What does he need or want right now?* That new question helped me relate to him as a worthwhile human being. I began to listen, to observe, to open up my mind to new alternatives and solutions."

I was starting to fidget. "Look," I said. "What's the bottom line here? Maybe questions can help in small ways, but I need a major overhaul."

"I understand your impatience," Joseph said. "Bear with me while I take a guess at some of the questions you might be asking yourself right now." He had a mischievous gleam in his eyes. "Maybe you're wondering, 'What's this crazy guy, Joseph, up to? Is he off his rocker? What do his ideas have to do with saving my career?' " His face lit up with an elfin grin that wrinkled the smile lines at the corners of his mouth.

I had to chuckle. Joseph had caught me. Was the *inquiring coach* a mind reader, too?

"There's really just one lesson here—that depending on the questions we ask ourselves, consciously or not, we literally put ourselves either in Learner or Judger mode. And we're our most effective selves when we're in Learner."

"The message here is to pay attention to the questions we're asking. . . ."

"Yes. But don't be concerned if you take the Judger path for a while. When your observer self is stronger, you'll find it much easier to switch your questions and get back into Learner mode. That's where things open up again.

"Ben, it's not a question of whether we'll go to Judger. Being human, we always will from time to time. The real question is whether we'll dig our heels in and stay there. That's what really causes problems."

"It would be great to be like you and know how to do this," I interrupted, "but you've been doing it for years, and apparently you've got a knack for spotting Judger questions. I'm not sure I have what it takes."

"Ah, but it's easier than you think," Joseph said. "The signals for catching yourself in Judger are obvious once you know how to spot them. Your body and your moods will tell you. Remember what happened to me with the superintendent? I wasn't getting any place with him until I recognized that my own mood was getting in the way. As long as I held onto that Judger attitude, I could never be constructive.

"Later, he and I talked about the moods and attitudes we associated with Judger—*self-righteousness, arrogance, superiority,* and *defensiveness* headed up the list. Add to that the habit of putting others down—or putting ourselves down—and you've got a prescription for a real mess. The questions we ask ourselves, whether conscious or not, can either be our worst enemies, or our greatest allies. I've discovered that almost every time I get into negative moods, Judger questions and attitudes are involved. Realizing that, I can change my questions for a very different result."

"So you're saying my body tells me what my mind is doing? It even indicates the kinds of questions I'm asking?"

"In fact, yes," Joseph said. "Your body and mood send you messages long before your mind does. You just need to learn your body's language. Think of this as your very own, built-in early warning system."

Body language! Early warning system! This was too much. "I don't get it. I guess you have to show me," I said.

"Great," Joseph said. "You're a researcher. Let's do an experiment. I have a way for you to experience what I'm talking about. Check this out. I'm going to recite two different sets of questions. Your job is simply to notice how each one affects you. Pay attention to your muscles, your posture, your breathing, and what you're experiencing in different areas of your body."

He got up, walked over to the Choice Map again, and stood in front of the Judger Pit. "Ask yourself these questions:

Who's to blame?
What's wrong with me?
Why am I such a failure?

Change Your Questions, Change Your Life

How could I lose?

How can I prove I'm right?

How can I be in control?

Why are they so clueless and frustrating?

How did I get stuck with the worst team?

Why bother?"

As he recited these questions, my chest tightened up. My shoulders stiffened. I was clutching up like a rookie pitcher in the last minutes of an important game. I laughed uncomfortably, "I think I see what you mean. I definitely feel some tension here and there."

"I thought you might. Almost everyone I've done this experiment with has some kind of reaction. What are some words you'd use to describe how those questions made you feel?"

I shrugged. "Just slightly uncomfortable, I guess."

"How about something a little more specific?"

I could see that Joseph wasn't going to let me off the hook. He was really pushing me. I decided to be honest with him, though it wasn't easy admitting even to myself what I was feeling.

"Well," I began, "I feel like that guy in the Judger Pit, stuck, bogged down." I was stumbling around with this. I wasn't used to putting words to my feelings.

"I know this isn't easy," Joseph said, apparently noticing I was having trouble. "People in my workshops come up with a variety of words: Hopeless and helpless. Pessimistic. Negative. Depleted. Depressed. Uptight. Loser."

Joseph was right! Every one of those words struck a chord with me.

"As you learn to recognize these body feelings, moods, and attitudes, you're conditioning yourself to recognize when you've landed in Judger. Once you've become familiar with your observer self, you'll be able to zero in on what kinds of questions are getting you stuck. The more you can observe yourself, the more objective you become. Later on, I'll give you more tools for doing that. Then you'll be able to craft questions that carry you right into Learner territory. This way, you can have your feelings, rather than them having you. That's another benefit of mastering the art of QuestionThinking."

Intrigued, I imagined myself as an observer and took a deep breath. In just a few moments I pretended I was watching myself sitting there in Joseph's office. I noticed my feelings beginning to shift. The changes were very subtle at first. With Joseph's encouragement, I was more able to notice them. "Aha! It's like you were saying. I am gaining distance from those negative feelings."

"Now, let's check out the other path, what it's like to be in Learner," Joseph said. This time he walked over to a different part of the mural and stood under the Learner billboard. I think he asked me to breathe normally for a few seconds before going on.

"Okay, good!" Joseph said. "Now here's the other set of questions. Ask yourself:

What happened?

What's useful about this?

What do I want?

What can I learn?

What is the other person thinking, feeling, needing, and wanting?

How can this be a win-win?

What's possible?

What are my choices?

What's best to do now?"

Almost immediately I experienced a quiet excitement. My breathing got easier. I began feeling a willingness and openness I certainly hadn't felt with the previous list of questions. One thing was particularly noticeable—my shoulders relaxed. I hadn't felt like this in a long while.

"How's that?" Joseph asked, smiling.

"What a difference! I like it."

"What are some words you'd use to describe this second experience?"

"Open," I said. "Lighter. Upbeat. Curious. Optimistic. A little hopeful . . . maybe there are solutions to my problems after all."

"Good! Good," Joseph reiterated. "These feelings signal that you've moved into Learner mindset."

Up until this conversation, I had never paid much attention to the ways questions—even ones I didn't realize I was asking—directed my feelings and actions. So that must be what Joseph meant by QuestionThinking. What was it he'd said? *Thinking takes place as questions and answers.* How do you like that! I had always prided myself on being a strategic thinker. Now I was beginning to suspect I knew only half the story. If Joseph was right, those questions we ask ourselves could have a definite impact on our decisions and results.

"The lesson I'd like you to take away," Joseph said, "is this—that the kinds of questions we ask ourselves can stimulate curiosity, inspire us, open us to new discoveries, and move us in the direction of success—or they can drive us into despair, inactivity, and failure. With my superintendent client that day, we both had a breakthrough right after I recognized I was in Judger. I changed my questions and, of course, after that, everything shifted. Then I showed the superintendent a Choice Map. Nobody escapes the Choice Map!" Joseph grinned from ear to ear.

"But did the guy get it?"

"Oh, sure he did. In the end, he made an interesting comment. With the 'Judger agenda,' as he called it, 'the costs can be tremendous. The future would just be a recycled version of the past. And with the Learner program the power is on. The juice is flowing. You can actually make a new future for yourself.' "

Learner-Judger Questions

Judger	Learner
What's wrong?	What works?
Who's to blame?	What am I responsible for?
How can I prove I'm right?	What are the facts?
How can I protect my turf?	What's the big picture?
How can I be in control?	What are my choices?
How could I lose?	What's useful about this?
How could I get hurt?	What can I learn?
Why is that person so clueless and frustrating?	What is the other person feeling, needing, and wanting?
Why bother?	What's possible?

We all ask both kinds of questions, and we have the power to choose which ones to ask in any moment.

Joseph settled back into his chair. "What's going through your mind right now?" he asked.

"I just realized," I said. "If it weren't for Charles, I never would have gone down the Judger path in the first place. I could have pulled out of the Judger Pit on my own if it hadn't been for him. He's driving me nuts."

"Tell me about Charles," Joseph said, looking sincerely interested.

"He's second in command on the project team I head up . . . but he challenges everything I say. Maybe he's got a legitimate bone to pick with me. He was passed over for the position I got, and boy, does he resent it. I would, too, if I were in his shoes! He's a real know-it-all, picky and petty. He's out to sabotage me. That's the bottom line. And it looks like he's succeeding."

"When you think about Charles, what's the first question that pops into your mind?"

I chuckled. "That's easy! *How can I put a leash on this guy before he destroys me?*"

"Anything else?"

"Lots of things! *How can I stay in control? How can I make this guy get with the program?*"

"And?"

"And . . . well . . . *How did I ever get myself into this mess? Whatever made me think I could handle this position?*"

Joseph responded. "Ask yourself, are these Learner questions or Judger ones? And depending on which they are, how might they impact your relationship with Charles?"

"Whatever you call them . . . they're what come up any time I think about him," I said.

"Yes, I understand," Joseph said. "However, is it Charles bringing you down, or is it *what you do with what Charles does* that brings you down? He's going to do whatever he does, and each moment you make your choice. The question for you is this: When Charles does his thing, are you going to choose Learner questions or Judger ones?"

"What are you talking about?" I snapped back. "The guy's an absolute jerk. What am I supposed to do, ignore the fact that he stabs me in the back every chance he gets?" I was getting plenty steamed. "There's no way to separate my reactions from what Charles does!"

"Ah, but that's the beauty of it," Joseph said. "You *can* separate your reactions from his behavior—and anyone else's. Until you do, you keep giving away your power. You're just a puppet. Anybody can pull your strings."

That really irked me! All my life I'd prided myself on being in control. My first reaction was that Charles wasn't the only one out to get me. Now it was Joseph, too. *What was he trying to prove? What did he have against me? What had I done for Joseph to go after me like this?* I felt defensive and self-righteous. And then it hit me. I'd taken a giant leap into Judger, just as Joseph had done with the superintendent.

"I'm not agreeing or disagreeing with you," I said, silently seething inside. "I can't imagine how I could possibly see this differently."

"Is that a question?" Joseph asked.

"What are you saying?"

"Can you reshape that statement as a question?"

"You mean, like, 'How might I see this differently'?"

"Exactly. Did you notice? You just switched into Learner. Quick as that. And here's my answer: No matter what Charles might do, the Choice Map, and what you're learning about your body's messages, will help you stand back and observe whether you're in Judger or Learner. You've empowered your observer self, so you can watch your own movie for a moment. Then you'll be able to tell the difference between what Charles does and *what you choose to do with what he does.*"

I tried to take in Joseph's statement. It wasn't easy. Judger questions were still running in my brain.

"Go back for a moment to that little guy standing at the crossroads," Joseph said, pointing at the Choice Map. "Remember, he represents everyone of us when we're hit with something we have to deal with. He's stumped. He's got two immediate choices. Know what they are?"

I nodded, pleased that I did know. "He can pause and check into those basic body feelings and moods associated with Judger and Learner," I said. "They'll tell him where he stands with himself—which kinds of Self-Q's he's asking. He can choose . . . he has choices."

That point really set off fireworks in my mind. I was beginning to see that Joseph was giving me some practical tools, not just criticizing my actions. "I have to say," I told him. "Maybe it's not as difficult to distinguish between Judger and Learner as I thought."

Joseph actually applauded. "Yes. Yes, that's great! Once you're able to observe your own thinking, and recognize the difference between Learner and Judger, you grab hold of the power of choice." Joseph seemed tremendously excited by this notion. "You're a quick study," he exclaimed. "I see another of the traits Alexa values in you so much." He glanced at his wristwatch. "It's a little after

Change Your Questions, Change Your Life

one o'clock now. Let's stop here for the day and resume tomorrow morning."

On the way out, Joseph stopped to pull something from a drawer. It was a white binder with a big red question mark on the cover. He explained that this was the QuestionThinking Workbook—the system of tools and lessons that he'd be showing me how to use in our time together. Then he pulled open another drawer, took out a copy of the Choice Map, and handed it to me.

"Take these with you," he said. "Study the Choice Map when you get to your office. Later you can put it in your binder. First, I want you to promise you'll take it home and post it on your refrigerator."

I groaned inwardly. *What on earth would I tell Grace about all this?*

As we walked down the hall Joseph summarized some of the things we'd discussed. "Here's your focus for now," he said, "Remember, the questions we form in our minds shape our decisions and actions and lead to any results we get. They put us on one of two paths, the Learner path or the Judger path, and there's a huge difference between them. QuestionThinking tools like the Choice Map and the distinctions between Learner and Judger questions give you the ability to recognize what kind of questions you're asking and where they might take you. If it doesn't look like they're taking you where you want, reshape them so they do. Think Learner and Judger questions. That alone can make a tremendous difference in your life. We're talking about core self-management skills here—ones that apply in your relationship with yourself and everybody else."

I heard Joseph telling me all this, but truthfully most of my attention was on Grace and my fears about what she'd think. Frankly, I was glad I was going to a late meeting, which meant I wouldn't have to put the Choice Map on the refrigerator until after she went to bed. At least I wouldn't have to deal with this until tomorrow.

At the double doors, Joseph stopped and I turned to face him. Over his shoulder, on the wall behind him, I saw a picture of Alexa. It appeared to be from a major magazine, profiling her for some award. Embarrassed though I was to admit it, I hadn't known about this article. Given how long I'd known Alexa I certainly should have.

"See you tomorrow," Joseph announced briskly.

My head was spinning. My whole life was being turned upside down. I hardly knew where the floor was anymore. What really puzzled me was that I also felt lighter, more optimistic than I'd been in ages. One thing Alexa was right about—this Joseph guy had a provocative way of looking at how to make changes in our lives. I began to imagine that maybe, by working with him, I'd come up with answers that would put my career back on track.

Kitchen Talk

*E*arly the next morning, awakened by the smell of fresh coffee, I made my way downstairs to the kitchen. Grace is always up before me. She's one of those people who wakes up cheerful and enthusiastic about each new day. I'm just the opposite. Grace claims that in the morning I'm like a bear coming out of hibernation. I don't think I'm quite that bad, but I don't exactly start the day off with a song in my heart.

As I entered the kitchen, I found Grace standing in front of the refrigerator with her back to me. She appeared to be engrossed with the Choice Map. I was immediately worried about what she might say. I was pretty sure she'd start probing and I'd have to tell her the whole thing—about my trouble at work and all the rest of it. That would lead to how I'd gotten the Choice Map and why I'd posted it on the refrigerator door. Then I might have to tell her about Joseph.

While I was thinking about how I would avoid telling her the whole story, Grace suddenly turned around and gave me a big hug. This startled me, especially since I'd expected her to still be upset after our confrontation at the airport the day before.

"Where did you get this?" she asked. "It's terrific!"

She had taken the Choice Map off the refrigerator door and was waving it around in her hand. I mumbled something about it being a handout for some special training at work. I poured a cup of coffee for myself and one for Grace.

"I'm amazed," she said. "I've already learned something from this. You remember Jennifer, at my office? I guess I've been riding her pretty hard lately. I can just feel her cringing any time I get within a few feet of her. Looking at this map, I realize I've been a real Judger with her, like it says here. She's been messing up a lot, but this makes me wonder if I've been contributing to the problem."

"It's all in the kinds of questions you ask," I said, sounding like an expert, which I definitely was not. I didn't even think before the words just popped out of my mouth. I checked myself immediately, realizing I sounded like

Joseph. Here I was freely talking about something that moments before I'd been nervous about sharing with Grace. What could I say next? I certainly wouldn't be able to explain much more about Joseph's ideas.

"What questions?" Grace asked. "I don't ever get that far with poor Jennifer."

"According to this guy Joseph, who invented this map . . ."

"Wait," Grace interrupted. "Who's Joseph?"

I stared at her blankly for a moment, debating about whether to tell her the truth. I decided to keep things simple. "He's this consultant Alexa hired," I told her, determined not to go into any more details than absolutely necessary. "He claims that most of the time we're not even aware of the questions we ask either ourselves or other people. That's what the Choice Map teaches us. It's a reminder to look at those questions."

Grace looked puzzled. I pressed close to her and pointed to the little guy at the crossroads. "There's the key right there," I said, pointing to the words, *Thoughts, Feelings, Circumstances,* around the character's head. "The moment anything happens to us, that's when we start asking questions. The sooner we recognize what we're asking, the better. That way we have more options." *Was this really me talking?* I was amazed at how much I recalled of Joseph's teachings.

"The main thing I see are these two paths," Grace

said, tracing first one and then the other with her finger. "Take the Learner route and you'll move right along. See. This guy is saying, 'What do I want? What are my choices?' This guy is asking, 'What can I learn?' Oh, you're right, these are all questions. And the guy on the Judger path, he's all caught up with other questions like, 'Who's to blame? What's wrong with them?' I'll tell you, Ben, at the office, every time I hear a pin drop or somebody sigh, the first thing that pops into my head is, 'Oh, Lord, what's wrong now? What can Jennifer possibly mess up today?' And then, in a flash, I'm down on her. Do you know what she did yesterday, Ben? She . . . Oh, hold it. That's taking me right into Judger territory, isn't it?"

"The way it works," I explained, "is that from moment to moment, stuff happens. Good stuff and bad stuff. It sort of hits us unawares. Then, if we have an inclination to be in Judger, our questions tend to follow that same pattern. If we're more in Learner, we'll ask questions in that direction."

"Action follows thought," Grace added. "It's a basic principle. But I never thought about it in terms of questions. Action follows questions. Seems to me the trick is to just keep ourselves in a Learner frame of mind."

I was thoroughly surprised by how far our conversation had gone and how easily Grace was catching on. I was even more surprised I remembered so much about what Joseph had been teaching me. I wasn't sure I had it right, but it seemed pretty close. The fact that the map had worked for Grace, and so quickly, was pretty good evidence that Joseph's ideas were right on.

"According to Joseph," I told Grace, "it's natural enough to slip into Judger now and then. In fact, we alternate between the two mindsets all the time. It's just human nature." Even as I said those words, I was thinking about my wife and those awful moments at the airport yesterday morning. I wasn't ready to go into all that with her, but at least I summoned up the nerve to mention part of it.

"Yesterday, I was trying to pull out into traffic and nearly got hit by a taxi that was going about twice the speed it should have. It was like a bolt of lightning, you know? It happened that fast. In an instant, I was ready to punch the guy out, cursing him under my breath."

"Sometimes you really worry me," Grace said, shaking her head.

My shoulders tensed up and I was on the verge of defending myself. I knew she didn't approve of my driving habits, though I'd never had an accident. We'd gotten into arguments about this, but a part of me said, *Don't go there this morning. Things are going so well right now. Don't spoil it.*

"It's just an example," I said. "That close call put me in Judger right away. I'm not saying I handled the whole thing so well. I was angry as hell. But later I did recognize what had happened, that I went into Judger in an instant. Seeing that was new for me."

I wanted to tell Grace the whole story, about how I'd lumped together everything I'd been experiencing that morning. I'd been stewing about whether or not to resign. I was irritated about having to meet with Joseph. I was hurting, worried about my whole career going up in smoke, and angry with Grace for pressuring me about our relationship in the midst of all this. It all became just one big . . . well, one big Judger Pit, I guess, and I had been sinking in the mud.

As these thoughts crossed my mind, a light went on in my brain. It was totally clear what path I had been on. It sure wasn't the Learner one! I realized I'd been as much of a challenge to Joseph as that judgmental superintendent he told me about. I'd slouched into his office, certain that meeting with him was a hopeless waste of my time. In the mood I'd been in, it was a miracle anything he said had gotten through to me. Now I was telling Grace all about it, as if I actually knew what I was talking about!

"I'm thinking this map is a good reminder of what happens to me when I get stuck in one of my Judger-heads," Grace said. She turned away for a moment and sat down at the breakfast table. She sipped her coffee and nibbled toast as she studied the map more closely. I poured myself a bowl of cereal and milk and sat down across from her. After a moment, Grace looked up a little shyly.

"Maybe this could help us. You know, our relationship," she said. "What do you think?" There was not the slightest hint of blame or judgment in her voice. I was really grateful for that.

"Joseph says that life is filled with those moments when something hits us and sets us off on one path or another . . ."

"But what do *you* think," Grace asked, "I mean, about it helping us—you and me?"

This time there was a bit of an edge in her voice. She really wanted me to tell her exactly what I was thinking. "As I said," I answered. "I think it applies well to any and all areas of our lives. It's a pretty effective tool."

"What's that supposed to mean?" she said.

I tried to ignore Grace's eyes. So far our conversation had gone so well, I didn't want it to turn sour. I was already asking myself, *What stupid thing did I say to set things off in the wrong direction again?* And then I caught myself. That simple little question was pushing me right down the Judger path. This time, though, I saw it coming, and I remembered to change my question to one that would be helpful: *How can I keep this conversation positive?*

"Sorry," Grace was saying. "I just realized I was about ready to go Judger on you."

In spite of myself, I had to laugh. "Me, too," I said. "Me, too."

"What are you smiling about?" Grace asked.

"Sweetheart," I said, "I love you!" I took her in my

arms and held her close. "Do you remember three or four days ago, when I was late meeting you for dinner?"

I felt her nod her head against my shoulder.

"We really got into it, didn't we, about who got their times mixed up. Then you did an amazing thing. You just suddenly dropped the whole argument and everything shifted. Do you remember?"

"Mm hmm, I sure do!" She chuckled, planting a kiss on my cheek.

It was difficult being serious and remembering that amazing night, but I really wanted to get my point across. "Joseph talks about switching from Judger to Learner, and how we can do that with a single question."

"Like, if I ask myself *Do I want to win this argument or do I want to have a good time tonight?*" Grace drew away from me but kept her hands on my shoulders.

"Is that how you do your magic?" I asked.

"Some of it," she said, leaning into me again. "But I never thought of it in terms of questions."

"I'm serious," I said, still wanting to make sure I got my point across. "I just realized that you do the very thing Joseph talks about. You do it by changing your questions, even if you haven't been aware of it. That's how you shift your mood!"

"I like those shifts!"

"Me, too," I said, hugging her again. "How did you learn to do that?"

Before she could answer, the electronic timer chirped on the stove. Grace always sets it to alert her when it's time to get ready for work.

"Oh, no!" She sighed, suddenly all businesslike. "I'm sorry, Ben. I'd love to call in late but I really can't. There's an important meeting scheduled."

In the next instant, she was dashing up the stairs to take a shower and get dressed. Twenty minutes later she kissed me goodbye and raced out the door. When I got around to pouring myself another cup of coffee, I noticed the Choice Map was gone. Grace had taken it to work with her!

As I was getting in my car to leave for the office, I noticed a piece of paper stuck under the windshield wiper. It was a hurriedly written note from Grace:

Darling,

Thank you so much for the Choice Map—and especially for the good talk this morning. You can't imagine how much it meant to me!

> *I love you, Grace*

I hadn't expected Grace to take the Choice Map, but there was no harm done. I could get another from Joseph. Meanwhile, it looked as if I'd redeemed myself in her eyes, at least for now. Good! That was one less pressure in my life.

Seeing with New Eyes, Hearing with New Ears

5

*A*s I stepped off the elevator at the Pearl Building that morning, I found Joseph watering his ficus trees with a large red watering can. It surprised me to see him doing something I would have handed off to my staff. He turned to me with a friendly smile. "I love having plants around. It's a daily reminder that all living things require our attention," he said. "No office should be without at least a plant or two. My wife, Sarah, is the gardener in our family. She says plants force you to ask questions. Are they getting enough water, enough sun? Do they need a little pruning? Do they need special nutrients? They thrive on questions, just as human beings do." He quickly finished his gardening chores and we went inside.

"When we finished up yesterday, we were talking about the Choice Map and what it tells us about Learner and Judger," Joseph began. "Have you had any further thoughts about any of this?"

I guardedly told him about Grace, our talk in the kitchen that morning, and how she'd taken the Choice Map to work. He seemed pleased and handed me two more Choice Maps—one for the refrigerator, the other to put in my binder.

"It's clear that we get different results depending on which of the two roads we take—Learner or Judger," I told Joseph. "Maybe I get stuck in Judger more than I'd like to admit."

"You're not alone in that," Joseph said. "It's easy to get stuck. Fortunately, there's a fast track out of there. Look at this road in the middle." Joseph pointed to the little road joining the Judger and Learner paths. It was labeled the *Switching Lane*. "That lane is the key. Let me show you how it provides such a powerful tool for switching from Judger to Learner.

"When you're standing in Judger," Joseph continued, "the whole world can look pretty bleak. As my client the superintendent said, when we're in Judger, the future can only be a recycled version of the past."

"Ouch!" I said. "One thing for sure, I couldn't stand to go through these past few weeks again!"

"Look at it this way," Joseph continued. "Even though the world is filled with infinite possibilities, you have only limited access when seeing with Judger eyes or hearing with Judger ears. Let me show you how to stand in a different place and change your viewpoint, how to give yourself new eyes and ears, sometimes almost instantly. For a moment, put yourself back on the Judger path at the start of the Switching Lane."

I turned my attention to the map and located the place he indicated.

Seeing with New Eyes, Hearing with New Ears

"Any time you step onto this path," he continued, pointing to the Switching Lane, "you automatically step into choice. You unveil a whole new picture of what's possible. You wake up; you've switched on your Learner eyes and ears. That's where QuestionThinking gives you the power to choose. When you can observe your own thoughts, especially Judger ones, you gain the ability to choose what to think next. If you can't observe what's already present, you stay in the dark."

"You're talking about choice like it's something we possess . . . a capacity."

"Absolutely! We're all born with that capacity," Joseph exclaimed. "That's what makes us human. Choice is ours, although it takes practice, and sometimes courage, to make best use of it. The author and concentration camp survivor Viktor Frankl spoke of '. . . the last of the human freedoms— to choose one's attitude in any given set of circumstances, to choose one's own way.' That's the essence of QuestionThinking."

"As much as this might compute for me," I said, musing on this last statement, "*applying* it is another matter altogether."

"Of course," Joseph responded. "making this *practical* is what it's all about. It's where the rubber hits the road. Here's a quick exercise to get you started: Whenever you sense you might be in Judger, pause, take a deep breath, and ask yourself, *Am I in Judger?* If your answer is yes, you can step onto

Change Your Questions, Change Your Life

the Switching Lane by asking simple questions like: *How else can I think about this?* and *Where would I like to be?"*

"Is it really that easy?"

Joseph laughed. "It's not always easy, but it is simple. A certain kind of question takes you there—what I call *Switching questions.* These questions put you on the Switching Lane—and pretty quickly you're on the Learner Path. You'll find a list of Switching questions in your binder. That list is another of the tools in the QT system."

Joseph paused and gazed thoughtfully out the window. "Let me tell you a story that clearly illustrates how Switching questions work. It's a true story about my daughter Kelly, who's an avid gymnast. She was so good that in college, she started training for the Olympics.

"Here's what happened. While Kelly was training for the Olympic tryouts, she'd perform quite well most of the time, but only *most* of the time. Sarah and I knew she'd never make the team that way. Her performance was too erratic.

"So we worked with her. We asked her to focus on what she had on her mind moments before any performance. She discovered she always asked just one basic question: *Will I fall this time?"*

"Which is a Judger question," I observed.

"Right," Joseph said. "And asking it produced what my daughter calls *Judger mischief.* That question really interfered with her performance. So the three of us worked on finding a Switching question she could ask herself instead, one that would propel her quickly into Learner. What she came up with was, *How can I do this routine beautifully?* That did the trick. Using that new question, Kelly reprogrammed herself by directing her attention in a positive direction. Her performance improved exponentially and also became highly predictable. Kelly says that new question helps her stay in *the zone.*"

"Did she make the Olympics?"

"She sure did," Joseph said. "And by the way, she came home with a bronze. I can't tell you how proud I am of her, though I have to confess that twenty years ago, I would have probably chastised her for not bringing home the gold. Oh, I tell you, having children teaches us to ask a whole new set of questions! By the way, you'll find Kelly's story in my *QuestionThinking Hall of Fame.*"

"This all sounds like a bit of magic, to me," I quipped. "Or a miracle."

"It's neither magic nor a miracle," Joseph said, smiling. "It's a *method*—practical tools that take advantage of how humans work. Questions always direct our attention. New questions can redirect our attention. They change assumptions and what we see as possible in any moment. Questions can even change us physiologically. For example, the question *What if I get fired?* can set off a whole chain of stress reactions in your body. Kelly's question, *Will I fall this time?* actually produced anxiety, which contributed to her old programming for failure. Consciously, of course, she didn't want that, but it's what happened anyway. *Thought sets intention.* Learner questions program us with a positive intention—in Kelly's case, for the right attitude and moves for an outstanding performance."

"Your implication is that Judgers can't be top performers," I argued. "I can't agree with you there. I've known Judger types who produced quite a lot."

"There are certainly people who spend more time in Judger than Learner," Joseph said. "And they may be quite driven and productive. But they can also drive everyone around them nuts, lowering productivity, cooperation, creativity, and people's ability to contribute. Operating from Judger can build resentment and conflict, whether with your family or your co-workers. An organization run by people in high Judger tends to have greater levels of stress, conflict, and problems with staff. And imagine the havoc Judger plays when you take that mindset home with you at night!

"Sarah once wrote an article called, 'Judger Marriage, Learner Marriage: Which Kind Is Yours?' for a major magazine. Her premise was that our experience of intimate relationships will be very different depending on whether we look on our partner with Learner eyes or Judger eyes. We expanded that idea into a book we wrote together just last year, titled *The Inquiring Marriage.* Sarah points out that with Learner we focus on what's working in our relationship and what we appreciate about the other person. We build

Seeing with New Eyes, Hearing with New Ears

from strengths rather than dwelling on flaws—our own or our spouse's. Does this make sense to you, Ben?"

I nodded, silently realizing that if this were true I had better start applying these lessons with Grace.

"In Judger, whether at home or work, everything can begin to look like one big headache. Nobody seems to be cooperating. Everything's a roadblock. When that happens we need to go back to some of the basic Switching questions: *Am I in Judger? Is this where I want to be? Will it get me what I really want?* Pause, take a deep breath, put yourself on the Switching Lane, and step right up to the Learner Path."

"If what you say is true, I could just stay in Learner by always keeping those questions in mind."

"Theoretically, yes. But life really isn't that simple. And not one of us is a saint. We're all going to fall into Judger from time to time," Joseph said. "It's just human nature. In fact, we probably do it every day. But I can promise you this—the more you use the Choice Map, Switching questions, and other tools I'm going to give you, the faster you'll be able to step into Learner, the easier it will be, and the longer you'll be able to stay there. You'll also spend less time in Judger, and the consequences of being there will be minimized. But *never* go Judger? Nope. There'll never be a time when you're permanently in Learner. And if you think you are? Well, you're just fooling yourself."

I had to push back on some of this. So I told Joseph, "This is beginning to sound like exercising any kind of judgment will send us down the wrong path. There are times when judgment is critical. For example, when hiring a new employee or buying a new home."

"I'm glad you brought this up. It's an important point. Take note, Ben. Being in Judger is *not* the same as using good judgment. The way I'm using the word, Judger always means *judgmental*. It's a form of attacking either others or ourselves. By contrast, exercising good judgment means making wise choices based on sound information and intentions."

"Okay, that makes sense."

"Here's another point that's absolutely vital for using the QT system powerfully," Joseph continued. "Judger has two faces. One focuses on being judgmental toward *ourselves*, whereas the other focuses on being judgmental toward *others*. The results can look quite different but they come from that same judgmental place."

"Okay," I said slowly. I certainly had been experiencing exactly what he described—feeling judgmental toward others but also getting pretty down on myself.

"If we focus our Judger mindset on ourselves, for example, with questions such as *Why do I always mess up?* we'll tend to feel depressed and diminish our self-confidence. On the other hand, if we focus our Judger mindset on others, with questions such as *Why is everyone around me so clueless and frustrating?* we tend to get angry, resentful, and hostile. Either way, Judger usually puts us in conflict.

"Let me give you an example of doing Judger to ourselves. Years ago, my wife, Sarah, was talking with Ruth, her editor at one of the magazines she writes for. They discovered they both had issues with their weight. Sarah told Ruth how she used the Choice Map to help her make better choices about food. Ruth got excited and asked Sarah to write an article about it.

"In the article, Sarah wrote about the questions we ask ourselves when we've eaten something we know is going to pack on the pounds—*What's wrong with me? Why am I so out of control? Why am I so bad?*"

"Those are all judgmental questions," I interjected.

"Yes. And whenever Sarah got into those Judger questions, she really beat herself up, which of course sent her spiraling right down to the Judger Pit. Then she often ate even more. Once she discovered she was asking those *troublemaker* questions, she decided to look for Switching questions to rescue herself. She came up with two: *Am I willing to forgive myself?* and *How do I want to feel?*"

"Which got her onto the Switching Lane?" I was starting to get the knack of Joseph's system.

"Right again. Once she switched into Learner, she developed questions for staying there: *What will serve me best right now? Am I being honest with myself? What can I do to feel better that doesn't involve eating?* Whenever she asked herself one of these questions, she felt empowered rather than out of control. Not only that, she's gotten herself in great shape. Even better, she tells me it's pretty easy to maintain that now."

Judging by the photos of her on Joseph's desk, Sarah certainly didn't look like a woman with weight issues. But all this talk was making me even more uncomfortably aware of how often the questions I asked myself were straight out of Judger mindset.

"From what I've seen so far," Joseph said, in an amazingly accepting tone of voice, "while you obviously don't have trouble with your weight, you still have a lot of self-Judger going on."

"I can't disagree," I hedged. "But what's your basis for saying that?"

"That's easy," Joseph said. "Yesterday, you were certain I saw you as a Judger and loser."

"Go on," I said hesitantly, worried that I was stepping into something I would regret.

"That perspective keeps you bogged down. But while you aim judgmental questions at yourself," Joseph said, looking straight at me, "you're also pretty good at targeting other people."

"I agree I can be pretty hard on myself. But on other people? I don't think so." I began to squirm. "Sometimes people really are jerks and idiots. I know I'm right about that. You've got to accept this as a fact of life and exercise good common sense, or good judgment, as you already said."

Without comment, Joseph directed my attention

back to the Choice Map. As I held it in my hand, he leaned forward and pointed at the figure who was starting down the Judger path. Then he pointed to the bubble over his head. It contained just one question, which I read out loud, "Who's to blame?"

Immediately I started thinking about the problems I'd run into over the past few weeks. I focused on that awful moment when I concluded I'd never make it and would have to resign. I was certainly in my Judger-head at that moment, having judged myself as a loser. But wasn't I justified? I couldn't deny I'd screwed up.

"What's going on with you right now?"

I replied with discomfort, "The more we talk, the more I see I've got to accept the blame for a lot of what's happened."

"Blame," Joseph said. "Tell me exactly what that word means to you."

"The bottom line? It means I should step down. I'm the incompetent one here. Period. End of conversation."

"Back up for a moment. Change your question from 'Who's to *blame*' to 'What am I *responsible* for?'"

I thought about this for a moment. "Blame. Responsibility. Aren't they the same thing?"

"Not at all," Joseph said. "Blame is Judger. Responsibility is Learner. There's a world of difference between them. If you ask questions about who's to blame, you block yourself and others from finding alternatives and solutions. It's very hard to fix a problem when operating from Judger blame. Blame can paralyze you. On the other hand, if you focus your questions on what you're responsible for, you open your mind to productive action. You're free to create alternatives and remedy the situation."

I was stuck on that word, *paralyze*. I felt an urge to get up, stretch, and walk around. I took a break, went to the restroom, splashed some cold water on my face.

"Remind me what you said about Charles yesterday," Joseph said, after I returned.

Ah, back to Charles! Now I knew I was on solid ground. It would be easy to prove to Joseph how my good judgment served me in this case, that my feelings about Charles were not just the product of Judger attitudes. "I told you, if it weren't for Charles I wouldn't be in this mess," I said. "That's obvious. He's playing a win-lose game. You'd have to be blind not to see that."

Without replying, Joseph directed me to turn to my binder and the chart inside. It was labeled *Learner-Judger Chart: Mindsets and Relationships*. I studied it for a moment, checking out the two columns that listed key characteristics of Learner and Judger. Those two columns were very different. It hit me immediately how one way of thinking would take me down the Judger path while the other would draw me up in the Learner direction.

"This chart provides a way to become a much better observer of ourselves." Joseph said. "It lists Learner and

Seeing with New Eyes, Hearing with New Ears

Learner/Judger Chart

Mindsets

Judger	Learner
Judgmental (of self and/or others)	Accepting (of self and others)
Reactive and automatic	Responsive and thoughtful
Know-it-already	Values not-knowing
Inflexible and rigid	Flexible and adaptive
Either/or thinking	Both/and thinking
Self-righteous	Inquisitive
Afraid of difference	Values difference
Personal perspective only	Considers perspectives of others
Defends assumptions	Questions assumptions
Possibilities seen as limited	Possibilities seen as unlimited
Primary mood: protective	Primary mood: curious

We all have both mindsets, and we have the power to choose where we operate from in any moment.

Relationships

Judger	Learner
Win-lose relationships	Win-win relationships
Feels separate from others	Feels connected with others
Fears differences	Values differences
Debates	Dialogues
Criticizes	Critiques
Listens for:	Listens for:
Right/wrong	Facts
Agree/disagree	Understanding
Differences	Commonalities
Feedback perceived as rejection	Feedback perceived as worthwhile
Seeks to attack or defend	Seeks to resolve and create

We all relate from both mindsets, and we have the power to choose how we relate in any moment.

Judger qualities and characteristics, and therefore provides clues for discerning where we are at any moment. It's invaluable for helping us shift from Judger to Learner. Try a little experiment now. Think about Charles. Then read off the words or phrases on the chart that immediately leap to your attention."

"*Reactive and automatic. Know-it-already. Listening for agreement or disagreement. Self-righteous...*" I stopped. Everything I was reading was in the Judger Mindset column. My jaw tightened. Then I turned to the *Learner Mindset* column. Only one phrase caught my eye: *Values not-knowing.* I was puzzled.

"I'm not sure what you mean by *values not-knowing,*" I said.

"Think about when you're doing research," Joseph explained. "You want to discover something new, which is impossible if you're attached to thinking you already know the answers. Valuing not-knowing is the basis of all creativity and innovation. It's the state of mind that's open to all kinds of possibilities, of looking for something new, something that might even be surprising. Instead of defending old opinions or interpretations, you're looking with fresh eyes."

I could apply that to myself when I was doing technology work, when my questions drew me into areas I wanted to learn about. Beyond that, especially with relationships, I felt like I was in foreign territory. Suddenly, I was confused. Was it Charles or me who was *reactive and automatic? Was it him or me who was a know-it-already? Who was it that was listening for agreement or disagreement? Who was self-righteous?* Was I as stuck in Judger as Charles?

Seeing with New Eyes, Hearing with New Ears

Before I could recover from my confusion, Joseph hit me with something else. "Now I want you to think about something with serious implications. What do you think are the *costs* of spending time in the Judger Pit?"

That question hit me like a thunderbolt. I hadn't seen this one coming at all! By now, I recognized that being in Judger slowed down my work, and that communicating with other people was becoming increasingly challenging—for them *and* for me. I wasn't able to admit it to myself back then, yet in retrospect I knew that whenever I got mired in the Judger Pit my whole department nearly ground to a halt. I was surrounded with evidence for how badly things were going. Joseph's question about Judger costs forced me to look at the whole situation more honestly.

I told him grimly, "It's a tough one. I've really let Alexa down. I've let everyone down. As for Grace and me . . ." I stopped. This was too difficult to say out loud. I knew I had been withdrawing from her—even pushing her away. Truly, I had only been trying to hide what was really going on with me. I was so sure she'd do what my first wife did many years before—which was divorce me for being a loser, at least in her mind.

"Are you okay?" Joseph asked.

"I'm all right, I guess," I responded. "But this sure isn't easy. I don't even want to think about the cost to the company for my having been so Judger. First of all, I'm getting a pretty good salary, but it's money down a black hole in terms of what I'm producing. On top of that, I'm sensing that I've created a no-win situation that has brought my whole team down. I dread going to team meetings. And the trickle down to other departments we work with . . . well, this isn't a pretty picture! If it goes on like this, we'll never meet our deadlines."

Joseph was nodding, apparently satisfied with my insights. "This is a big breakthrough," he told me. "You're doing great, Ben."

"Great? What are you talking about? This is a disaster. Throw me a lifeline, would you? How do I get out of this?"

"I *could* drag you out," he said, "but I'm going to give you something even more valuable—tools to get yourself out. I want you to recall a time when you were in Learner in a work situation, really solidly there. Recall as vividly as you can what that experience was like. If you have trouble remembering, take a look at the Learner side of the chart."

Right away I recalled my best work at AZ Corp, how everything flowed, how I really enjoyed coming to work. My productivity was high. The productivity of the people around me soared. In contrast to what I was experiencing at QTec, people enjoyed working with me, though as a researcher I spent a lot of time alone.

"With technology problems I have tests to determine whether an idea is likely to work or to cause problems. You know, if you plug a six-volt motor into a thirty-volt circuit, something's going to blow. With the right tests you can avoid ruining an expensive piece of equipment."

"I see what you mean," Joseph said. "Applying these same principles to your work with the team might be a challenge, however. Humans aren't quite that simple."

"That's what Grace keeps telling me," I said.

We both chuckled.

"So let me see if I understand you correctly," Joseph said. "In your approach to technology problems, it's easy for you to stay in Learner. You're really good at that. You have specific questions that help you step outside yourself, to make objective choices."

"You could say that, yes."

"Great. I have good news for you. This is going to be simpler than you think. You already have the basic thinking skills. I'm just giving you new tools to take advantage of them in another area, in communicating with other people. Everything we've been discussing provides you with a similar method for handling people situations. The Choice Map gives you a mental picture of the difference between Learner and Judger ways of behaving and relating. There's learning to recognize how the kinds of Self-Q's you ask set you off on one path or another. Then there's the Switching Lane, Switching questions, and the Learner-Judger Chart that helps you pinpoint where you are and make new choices about where you want to go. Equipped with these key tools to recognize Judger, distinguish it from Learner, and switch to Learner whenever you choose, you're well on your way to making the changes you want in your life."

"Joseph," I said, "you're beginning to get through to me. But isn't there a way to just free myself of Judger mindset once and for all?"

"Oddly enough, that's the irony, you free yourself from Judger by accepting it as part of you."

"Huh? How can I be free of something that's part of me?"

"It does sound like a contradiction, doesn't it," Joseph said. "But we can all exercise this kind of acceptance. And only by doing this can we truly gain the freedom to choose. Let me tell you a story to clarify this principle. It also illustrates the potential costs of judging others. Did Alexa ever tell you about her husband Stan's breakthrough?"

"She mentioned it," I replied. "You helped him make a pile of money, as I understand it."

"He's very proud of that story," Joseph said. "He used the QT tools to earn his way into my *Hall of Fame*. Stan, as Alexa may have told you, is in the investment business. Here's the gist of his story.

"Some years back, Stan was a very judgmental guy but certainly didn't think of himself that way. If he had a run-in with someone, or heard gossip about them that wasn't flattering, he'd write them off. Stan will tell you that he clung to his assumptions like a snapping turtle. He turned down many business opportunities on the basis of rumor, idle gossip, and guilt by association. He justified it all as a way of minimizing risk—which was only partially true.

"He made a huge investment in a promising start-up company. About a year later, the company hired a CEO who'd been employed by a firm that was implicated in a big financial scandal. Although this guy had been exonerated of any wrongdoing, Stan insisted that where there was smoke there was fire. He was on the verge of pulling his money out but was also in a great deal of conflict about the whole thing. Except for the CEO they'd hired, the company seemed to be doing everything right.

"About this time, Sarah and I had dinner with Stan and Alexa. We were discussing the Learner and Judger concepts, and Alexa encouraged Stan to apply it to evaluating his investment decision. She suggested he apply the *A-B-C-C Choice Process* to his quandary, and Stan agreed to try it out. Here's how that process goes:

"*A—Aware. Am I in Judger?* Stan was very funny about this. Having described the characteristics of Judger, Stan, amazingly, admitted that an awful lot of what we described applied to him. His response that night surprised us: 'Being in Judger is my forte!' We all laughed, though we knew he was beginning to look at his behavior more honestly.

"*B—Breathe! Do I need to step back, pause, and look at this situation more objectively?* Stan smiled at this question, took a deep breath, paused, and shortly admitted that

A-B-C-C Choice Process

A   **Aware**
Am I in Judger?

B   **Breathe**
Do I need to step back, pause, and look at this situation more objectively?

C   **Curiosity**
Do I have all the facts? What's happening here?

C   **Choose**
What's my choice?

he was anything but objective. He really distrusted this new CEO, though he'd never even spoken with the man.

"*C—Curiosity. Do I have all the facts? What's happening here?* We asked Stan if he'd done anything to collect objective information? Did he have everything he needed to make a responsible judgment? Stan realized that he'd never gotten past his distaste for what he'd heard about the guy. But facts? No, he actually had no facts.

"*C—Choose. What's my choice?* Well, by then Stan himself realized that he didn't have all the information he needed to make a wise choice. He owed it to himself to check out the situation.

"A month later Stan called to tell me he'd checked

around and found out the new CEO was a good guy. Long story short, Stan left his money in, the company went public two years later, and he made a fortune.

"The whole situation made Stan stop and think. Realizing how much it almost cost him to stay in Judger, now he consistently takes himself through the A-B-C-C Choice Process. None of this would have happened if he hadn't been able to accept the Judger part of himself. Using the Choice Process begins with acceptance, then builds on it. Stan was amply rewarded. He and Alexa bought a new vacation home just last week.

"If you met Stan today, you'd still notice that he's very opinionated and judgmental. He knows that part of himself very well. Now he accepts it and even laughs about it, but he doesn't allow it to blind him in making decisions."

"Great story!" I said, and I really meant it. I found the A-B-C-C formula in my binder and jotted down a few notes.

"Look at how much Stan and Sarah both changed just by examining the role Judger played in their lives," Joseph noted. "There are important differences, of course. Sarah was judging herself—that's *internal Judger,* while Stan was judging others—that's *external Judger.* There were very real costs, regardless of which Judger face was used. In both cases, the change they wanted was blocked."

"This all sounds great. It really does. But here's something I'm stuck on. Learner can sound soft. Leaders have to act tough and make the tough calls. I don't see how

Learner ways of operating can help me do that. How do I get past this?"

Joseph chuckled. "I was wondering if you would ask me that. This is the only real pushback I ever get on these theories. Do you think of Alexa as decisive?"

"Very," I responded, thinking back to some tough decisions she had made that I wouldn't have wanted to face myself.

"I agree with you. Now let me answer your question with another question. Can you fire someone from a Learner place?"

"Sure," I answered.

"Good. And what might be the consequence of firing someone when you're in a Judger state?"

"Maybe a lawsuit. Oh. Okay. Point made," I said as I absorbed this. Then I reflected, "Seems like life would be a lot simpler if we could all just recognize Judger in ourselves, switch to Learner, and operate from there."

"How true!" Joseph said. "That's the ultimate goal of the QuestionThinking system. Use the Choice Map, Switching questions, and the Learner and Judger distinctions daily. They show you how to observe yourself and the world around you, how to make wiser and more conscious choices. This isn't just a once-in-a-lifetime insight though. It's a *practice,* something you do daily. Use it or lose it! You'll soon have the ability to calmly and systematically recognize when you're in Judger—whether you're aiming it at yourself or someone else. Remember, it's about accepting Judger and practicing Learner. The benefits you'll gain from these keys will keep reinforcing themselves. Soon, everything you've learned will flow pretty easily; you won't even have to think much about it. You really will be seeing with new eyes and hearing with new ears."

Joseph glanced at his watch. "We've been talking quite a while. We can take a short break and then go on to the next step, or wait until the next time we get together. What do you want to do?"

I was torn. This had already been an intense day and I wanted to get out of there. I needed time to chew on what we'd covered so far. But frankly, I was a bit nervous about *not* hearing the rest of what Joseph would tell me. I knew that soon I would have to deal with costs and consequences of Judger where Charles and Grace were concerned. I looked up at Joseph with a lame smile and said, "Okay, let's go for it!"

"Great! I think you'll like what comes next."

Accept Judger,
Practice Learner

*W*hen we reconvened a half hour later, Joseph started the session with a story. He said, "You've probably heard of the mythologist Joseph Campbell. He was famous for coming up with exactly the right story for every situation. Here's one he told me, many years ago.

"It seems a farmer was out working his field when his plow caught on something and wouldn't budge. His first reaction, of course, was to go into what I've called Judger.

Cursing, he began digging around to free the plow. To his surprise, it was caught on an iron ring buried deep in the ground.

"After freeing his plow, the farmer got curious and pulled on the iron ring. Off came the lid of an ancient chest. Before him, glittering in the sun, lay a treasure of precious jewels and gold.

"This story reminds us that it is often by confronting our greatest obstacles that we find our greatest strengths and possibilities, but sometimes we've got to dig deep to find them. Campbell had a phrase for it: *Where you stumble, there your treasure is.* Finding the treasure will depend on your mindset and the questions you're asking, whether they're Learner ones or Judger ones."

"That might be fine and well. But I'm still not seeing how all this is going to help me. Where's the treasure in this mess of mine?"

Joseph easily took up my challenge. "You might start digging into that Judger question you just asked."

The moment he said this a light went on. "You mean, 'Where's the treasure in this mess of mine?' I guess I did mean that in a Judger way. But what's my alternative? It *is* a mess!"

"Is there another way of looking at your situation, Ben? Ask a Learner question."

I had to give that some thought. It wasn't easy coming up with a Learner question, but at last I did. "What might I learn from this situation?"

Change Your Questions, Change Your Life

"Great!" Joseph looked genuinely pleased.

"I'm not sure where to take it from here," I admitted.

"Let's do a little excavating then," Joseph said. "Let's look at how the kinds of questions you ask affect people around you, particularly your colleagues at QTec." He leaned back in his chair and took a deep breath. "How often are you in Judger when you meet with your team?"

"Truthfully? Just about every time lately!"

"And how would you describe your communication with them?"

"Communications? That's a laugh! Listen, I told you how awful our meetings are. When I do call a meeting nobody has much to offer. They sit on their hands and wait for me to tell them what to do. Finally I talk and Charles barrages me with his interminable questions. Doesn't matter what I say, he questions everything."

"When you're with your team," Joseph continued, "are you asking yourself the question, *How can I come up with the right answer?* or are you asking, *What can we accomplish together?*"

I felt confused. I wasn't sure exactly what I did but I knew it wasn't what Joseph was suggesting. "I guess you'll have to clue me in here."

"Okay. You've been in conferences with Alexa. How does she conduct her meetings? What does she say? What does she do?"

I always looked forward to Alexa's meetings. I told

Joseph, "Her meetings are invigorating. I come away with new ideas to pursue. I feel like charging back to my office to start acting on them. But I never could figure out what she does to produce that kind of excitement."

The moment those words were out of my mouth, it hit me. "Alexa asks questions," I said. "Her meetings are all about questions. But not interrogating kinds of questions. She really piques everyone's curiosity. Her questions motivate people . . . sometimes even inspire them."

"How are her questions different from yours?"

"Alexa has her style, I have mine," I said, feeling a little defensive.

"Do you ask questions?"

"Sure I ask questions. I ask my people what they've accomplished since our previous meetings. Or what they haven't, which is more accurate lately." I was starting to realize, even then, that my questions often put people on the spot.

"When your people give their answers, how do you listen? How do you respond?"

"It depends. If the answer is any good, I might jot it down. But lately, I leave those meetings with a blank pad."

"Describe what the experience of listening is like for you," Joseph said.

That wasn't difficult. "Mostly I've been pretty annoyed and impatient," I replied, "especially when a person's answer doesn't come close to solving the problem, or when it shows they're not following my plan. I get the impression nobody really cares."

"Check in with yourself right now. What's your attitude toward your co-workers? Are you in Learner or Judger?"

"What else! Judger, of course. But nobody is contributing a darn thing . . . if they would only . . ." I stopped. "Boy, I just stubbed my toe on that iron ring Joseph Campbell talks about, didn't I?"

"You sure did. Sharp observation. And like the farmer you immediately went Judger—which is a very common, human response," Joseph said. "So do what the farmer did after that. Get curious. Ask, 'What's happening here?' Follow the Learner path."

"Of course you would say that. But how do I do it?"

"Simple. You start by going into those meetings in Learner mindset. Try the kinds of questions I bet Alexa asks, like, *What are the goals of this meeting? How can we all get aligned on the agenda? How can I conduct the meeting to get the best from everyone? What might be valuable and worth considering from each person?* At the end, *Are we all on the same page with the action items we've come up with?*

"I'll bet you can figure out how those questions would change things. When you described Alexa's meetings, you answered that for yourself. They help create a Learner environment. That's key for building an effective team. By creating such an environment you encourage people—you included—to listen more patiently and carefully, seeking to understand rather than looking for what's right or wrong. You set the group up to get curious and ask Learner questions themselves, even when there are tough challenges."

"Right. It's the tough challenges part that gets me in trouble. We've got some big problems and nobody is willing to take them on. I've got to admit, that's where I get stuck. I go right into Judger."

"*Accept Judger, practice Learner.* Imprint that slogan in your brain. Think of it this way: You're never going to be pure Learner. But you can learn to make choices about where you put your attention. Whenever you give your attention to Judger you've got little energy left for anything else. You can just imagine how that's going to affect the people around you. Accepting Judger is step one for making a new choice—and that choice starts with switching to Learner questions. The end result is both personally satisfying and more productive."

"That's why Alexa's meetings are so great," I reflected. "They're Learner environments, like you say. I always have the sense that we have her full attention. If she ever goes Judger, I'm sure it's just for a fleeting visit." I had a sudden insight. "*All* she asks are Learner questions, and lots of them. I swear, you have the feeling that every word anyone utters is terribly important to her. I'll bet she also gets an almost perfect score on that 80/20 rule you told me about. You know, 80 percent asking, 20 percent telling."

"That's it," Joseph said. "When giving our full attention, we genuinely want to hear what people have to say. Alexa's listening is focused by questions such as: *What's valuable here? What's to be learned from that comment?* Not only does she ask Learner questions, she also listens with Learner ears. When we're able to listen from Learner, the impact on others is amazing. When people feel accepted, and not judged, they become much more forthcoming, cooperative, and creative. That's why the end result is that her teams turn into Learner teams very quickly. Remember the Choice Map, Ben? It's drawn to depict a single person but you can also apply all those exact same principles to teams—or even whole organizations."

I had to give this some thought. When I pictured the Choice Map, I could clearly see Alexa's whole team jogging happily along the Learner Path. Each of us was sent off on the journey by Learner questions. Our attention was free to focus on new solutions and possibilities. And what about my team? Most of them were down at the bottom of the map, wading around in the mud of the Judger Pit!

As difficult as it was to accept that Judger was my main *modus operandi* too, Joseph was right. It was becoming clearer by the moment why people wouldn't be real excited about working with me. "I'm just the opposite of Alexa," I mumbled. "She seems to create a Learner environment almost automatically."

"She wasn't always that way, I assure you. Like most

Accept Judger, Practice Learner

of us," Joseph noted, "she was automatically more Judger to start with. It takes effort and intention to turn the tide and become more naturally Learner. We're all evolving, Ben. If you're to claim your treasure, you'll need to literally and deliberately train your brain to do things it doesn't automatically know how to do on its own. I still practice this stuff myself every day."

"This is a lot to take in," I said. "When I first walked into your office, I was just looking for a quick fix. You're offering something a lot bigger."

Joseph nodded.

"Can't you narrow it down to a few words of advice?"

"How often do people really take advice?"

He was right, of course. "I guess I'm an expert at *not taking* advice." I grinned at my sudden insight.

"Aren't we all?" Joseph replied. "Good coaches avoid giving advice. Instead, they ask questions that help us find our own best answers. Like the digging necessary in the Joseph Campbell story, the best coaches guide us to our own treasures by asking us thought-provoking, even inspiring questions. Our best answers become our own best advice—which is the only kind most of us are likely to act on anyway."

"Accept Judger, practice Learner," I repeated once again, opening my binder to write down those words in bold letters an inch tall. "Joseph, that's the biggest jewel in my treasure chest right now. I can observe when I'm in

Accept Judger ? Practice Learner

Judger or Learner and make real choices about where I put my attention. I'm sure it will take me a while to put that lesson into practice consistently, but this gives me a great way to focus my efforts."

"Instead of trying to figure it out," Joseph suggested, "apply what you've learned to actual situations. That's the real test. It's where you'll find the most valuable treasure."

That's where we ended the session that day. Down on the street a few minutes later, I cut through the park across from the Pearl Building into an open playing field. An older boy was helping a younger one learn to ride a bicycle. I stopped to watch.

In spite of spills and near falls, they were having fun. There were shouts of encouragement, along with cries of despair as the younger boy made yet another mistake and tumbled to the ground. Each time the younger boy fell, the older one rushed to his side to give assistance and support to try again.

Finally, the younger boy caught on. He rode off, covering fifty feet or so, with the older boy chasing after him, whooping and hollering cries of victory. I caught myself thinking, *Why are adults so damned competitive? Why are they so uncooperative, always looking for a way to show up the other guy?* I was getting angry. I turned around to catch one last glimpse of the kids before getting into my car. Now the two of them were standing beside the upright bike, laughing together. I reached for the ignition and thought, *Wouldn't it be amazing if our team could work together like that? What a treasure that would be!*

At that moment I realized I'd done something quite new. I had made a Switch. I transformed a Judger question into a Learner one! And it had happened naturally. I couldn't wait to share this with Joseph. *Not bad,* I thought, *the inquiring coach is really onto something!* Suddenly, I wanted to find out what else he had up his sleeve. I was sure I'd discover more gems in my meetings with him. I was beginning to feel real hope that maybe it wasn't too late to salvage my career.

When the Magic Works

7

*O*ver breakfast the next morning, Grace told me about what had happened with Jennifer, the young woman at work she'd been having so much trouble with.

"I kept the Choice Map on my desk all day," Grace said. "Two Learner questions kept jumping out at me—*What do I want?* and *What are my choices?* When I applied those questions to Jennifer, I realized I wanted her to start exercising more common sense and initiative. So, I tried some new questions. I asked myself, *Why does Jennifer need so much direction from me?* I became truly curious about this. Was she afraid of acting on her own? Or worried that I'd fire her for making a mistake? To find out, the next time she came to me for help I asked her a question instead of just giving instructions. I asked her, 'How would you solve this problem if you were the boss?'

"That single question opened up a very productive conversation between us. Jennifer confessed that she was, indeed, afraid of me. She thought if she didn't do exactly what I expected her to do, I'd fire her. That talk changed everything between us. I think she feels more secure now. She's started working better on her own. She already appears to be taking more initiative. When it was time for her to go home, I congratulated her on her progress. She seemed pleased with herself, too.

"I'm really surprised . . . and glad. And, you know what? Asking questions made me feel a lot better at the end of the day—even a very challenging day. Ben, now I realize I was being unfair to Jennifer. I just assumed she was asking all those questions because she was incompetent. She really isn't. It's just that she believed she thought she had to check everything out with me."

I was glad Grace didn't ask me about any results I'd gotten from applying Joseph's ideas. Even though I'd had some shifts in my own thinking, I hadn't yet applied what I was learning in a real situation.

When I finally left the house I was at least twenty minutes late. Traffic was piling up on the freeway. A mile past my on-ramp, the freeway turned into a parking lot. Cars were lined up as far as I could see, four lanes wide. What an ordeal! I was getting frantic. I didn't even notice my Judger mindset kicking in. At least not right away.

I gritted my teeth, set the car in park, then got out my cell phone and checked for messages. My secretary had left several reminders. Only two stood out: a meeting with Alexa at nine thirty and one with Charles at eleven. I wasn't ready for either, least of all the latter.

I slapped the steering wheel in frustration, muttering something about how one guy, stupid enough to run out of gas, had ruined the whole day for half the city. *Who was the idiot responsible? I didn't need this! Didn't he realize. . .* I suddenly stopped myself. That's when I woke up enough to realize I was solidly in Judger! I actually laughed out loud. Then I heard sirens and an ambulance speeding along the emergency lane toward the front of the line. Accident! I switched on the radio for traffic news. Two people injured. I felt pretty foolish about jumping to the conclusion that some jerk had run out of gas.

Worries about the meeting with Charles kept intruding. I kept going around in circles with my anger toward him. I needed help on this one.

I remembered Joseph's counsel about changing my questions. I figured, what do I have to lose? I'd treat this situation as a trial run for applying his theories. But what kinds of questions would help me get out of what Grace labeled my *Judger-head?* What questions would help me move into Learner? I did realize I had already started on the Switching Lane since I must have asked myself, *Am I in Judger?* to notice that that was where I was.

Joseph suggested that when I caught myself in Judger I should stop, take a deep breath, then look at the questions I was asking myself at that moment. I did that. The first question that popped into my mind was about the traffic jam: *How can I get out of here?* Obviously, there wasn't much choice about that. I was stuck until traffic started moving again. Then something else Joseph said came back to me: *I can't always choose what happens, but I **can** choose how I relate to what happens.* Almost immediately, a new question came to mind: *How can I make best use of this time?*

It took only a second to come up with an answer to that one. I fished my wallet out of my pocket, took out Joseph's business card, and punched his number into my cell phone. He answered immediately.

"Ben here," I said. Do you have a minute? I'm stuck in traffic and going a little nuts."

Joseph was silent for a moment, then laughed: "Did you try saying 'beam me up, Scotty'?"

I laughed with him. I didn't think he was a Trekker, but I got his reference immediately. Laughing released some tension. My mood lightened considerably.

"I've got a meeting with Charles this morning," I explained. "I don't have the slightest idea what I'm going to tell him, but I know I'm still angry. I don't want to blow it. Where do I begin?"

"Good question," Joseph said. "I'm going to email you something I call *The Top Twelve Questions for Change.** Use it as a reference any time you're stuck, or frustrated, or want to make a change and you need a good Learner question. Meanwhile, can you write something down?"

"Sure," I said, grabbing my binder, which was on the seat next to me. Then Joseph dictated three questions from the Top Twelve list: *What assumptions am I making? How else can I think about this situation? What is the other person thinking, feeling, needing, and wanting?*"

Ben's Three Questions

1   What assumptions am I making?

2   How else can I think about this situation?

3   What is the other person thinking, feeling, needing, and wanting?

I looked at Joseph's first question: *What assumptions am I making?* That was a tough one. Sure, where Charles was concerned, I had definitely made some assumptions. They were unavoidable. I'd beat him out of a promotion he'd been counting on. Guys in that position can be dangerous. I'd be a fool to drop my guard with him. I was sure nothing would make Charles happier than to see me fail. Then he could step into my place and have what he wanted.

Some people might have called my judgments about Charles assumptions. Of course, an assumption isn't necessarily reality. That was something you learned early in engineering. But sometimes they do turn out to be real. My problems with Charles sure seemed real to me. Any fool could see he was intentionally undermining my authority by barraging me with questions whenever he had a chance.

Something was nagging at me. I had to ask myself, *was I defending my assumptions instead of questioning them,* like it says on the Learner-Judger Chart? I'd just gone through something like this with my assumptions about why traffic was stalled. I'd been so sure the traffic jam was caused by some idiot running out of gas. Yet it turned out I was wrong. Was it possible my assumptions about Charles were wrong, too? I made the decision to truly consider what I had been assuming about him.

Though agitated, I turned to Joseph's second question: *How else can I think about this situation?* Something Grace had said clicked in my mind. She described how her assumptions about Jennifer had negatively impacted her relationship with the young woman. Grace had used the Choice Map to find a different way of relating to Jennifer.

Could I do the same with Charles? *Was* there another way of thinking about him?

Because I had nothing better to do at the moment, I began to think about other possibilities. For example, what if I revised how I thought about Charles? What if I tried on the assumption that his questions weren't aimed at making me look bad at all? What if he just wanted to make sure we'd covered all our bases? The more I considered other ways of thinking about the situation, the less certain I was about my old opinions, and the better I felt about Charles.

I decided to try something new. When Charles walked in for our eleven o'clock meeting, I would attempt to suspend my assumption that he wanted to sabotage me. The moment this thought crossed my mind, new ideas tumbled into place. I wasn't ready to trust Joseph's theories 100 percent, but I knew I didn't feel quite so lost anymore. That was great. I actually had something new to *do*.

I was just starting to consider Joseph's third question—*What is the other person thinking, feeling, needing, and wanting?*—when traffic began to inch forward. I put that third question on hold. But even as I got under way, new possibilities began unfolding in my mind. If Charles was merely being inquisitive, what was he wanting or needing from me? I recalled a conversation we'd had my first day on the job. He'd said, "I have to tell you, I'm disappointed I didn't get that promotion. But I'll do everything I can to make this company successful. It's a great company and my family likes this town. I don't want to have to move." Maybe I'd overlooked some clues about Charles's intentions. I'd have to think about that.

I arrived at the office way behind schedule. With less than ten minutes before my meeting with Alexa, I flipped open my computer, went to a search engine, and typed in her name and the name of the magazine I'd seen in Joseph's *Hall of Fame* collection. The article about her popped up instantly.

Fast Company magazine had chosen Alexa for its *Woman of the Year* award. I scanned the story. It told about her stepping into the CEO position of a company that had already gone into Chapter 11. Everyone had advised her against it. They said it could destroy her career. She took the risk and accomplished the impossible. I skipped ahead several paragraphs. Alexa was quoted as saying she owed her success to "simply changing the kinds of questions I was asking." In the next paragraph she named her personal coach and mentor: Joseph. Who else?

Only moments later, seated in Alexa's office, I told her I'd read the article about her. "You never told me you got a *Woman of the Year* award," I said.

"Oh, yes," she sighed. "They labeled me *The Inquiring Leader.* You know what? I don't think they'd ever heard of a CEO asking questions. It was a great novelty to them!" She chuckled at the thought. "It seems like such a simple thing. Most leaders do more telling than asking.

That's why they never find out what's really going on. All too often they base their decisions about strategic direction, and even about their own people, on insufficient or inaccurate information."

"They make assumptions instead," I added, "which they never test."

"Exactly. Well, that just never made any sense to me." I heard Joseph's teachings in her words, but what she said was obviously authentic for her.

"Alexa, I'm curious about what happened at your old company. What were the Judger questions you started out with? What Learner questions turned things around for you?"

"You know, in retrospect it seems so easy I almost have to laugh. The kinds of questions we'd been asking were along the order of 'Who's to blame for the mess we're in?' I was lying awake nights trying to figure out whom I should fire—and worrying that it might be myself! Then, one day, talking with Joseph, I started coming up with new questions. I think the first one was, 'How can we avoid making so many mistakes?' Joseph liked that but suggested we change it to, 'How can we build on our successes?'

"That question did the trick. I got everyone on track with that new question. The Judger question had put us in a negative frame of mind. The Learner one piqued our curiosity and asked us to take positive and creative actions. Joseph said to use these new questions to build a Learner environment, and that's what I set out to do. Pretty soon we were turning things around in remarkable ways. Until this situation, I never realized the truth about the power of questions, that they can lead us either to failure or to success. It really was a big change for me, and for all of us."

"What was it about that new question that made such a difference?" I asked.

"The best way I can answer is with a story Joseph told us at the time. It had to do with a study that was done with two comparable basketball teams. Team A was coached with an emphasis on preventing mistakes on the court. Day after day, they reviewed videos that focused on their errors. Those mistakes got grooved in their brains. By contrast, Team B was coached with an emphasis on building from their successes. Day after day, they reviewed videos that focused on their successful plays. So Team B's successes got planted in their minds.

"To put it simply, Team A focused on what was wrong. Team B focused on what was right. I'm sure you can guess which team had the greatest improvement by the end of the season."

"The one that built on their successes, of course."

"That's absolutely right," Alexa said. "In fact, by the end, the difference in these teams' performances was startling. As I recall, Team A actually had a slight reduction in their accomplishments. Team B improved by nearly 30 percent. That's all it took to convince me of the power of asking the right kinds of questions. When I applied those same principles to our floundering company, dramatic changes began to occur almost immediately. Not only did our productivity increase but coming to work was more enjoyable, even fun. Creativity and mood were boosted. There was higher energy throughout the company. The whole place began operating on Learner principles, and it all happened in months instead of years. You know the rest of the story."

Alexa paused as she recalled that time of her life. "What could be more natural or obvious," she continued, "than to *simply ask*. How else can you hope to get a complete picture of what's going on? And how else can you get other people contributing so enthusiastically? Curiosity, genuine childlike curiosity, is one of our greatest assets . . . it's the fast track to Learner. How could we discover or learn anything without it? It's the fuel for so much change and growth!"

Curiosity: Fast track to Learner

I had to think about that. Joseph talked about curiosity, too. It was certainly as important to him as it was to Alexa. How could it really make a difference for me?

"What are you thinking, my friend?" Alexa was staring at me. "You're a million miles away."

When the Magic Works

I wasn't a million miles away at all. Actually, I had begun to think about Charles. If what Alexa and Joseph were showing me about the vital role of curiosity and Learner questions were true—well, maybe I really did have some rethinking to do. Were my Judger questions about Charles covering over something important? Before I had a chance to check myself, the words popped out of my mouth.

"He's asking because he's curious. He just wants to understand!"

Alexa looked at me with concern. "What in heaven's name are you talking about?"

"I was thinking out loud," I replied. "Maybe Charles has been asking all those questions to figure out where I was going, what I was expecting of him, and how come. I assumed he was making me wrong with all his questions. But what if he was just asking to make sure he was doing the right thing? What if he wasn't challenging my ability to lead? Those are real possibilities, aren't they? I really do need to take a new look at my assumptions about him. What is actually going on with him if he isn't, in fact, challenging my authority?" Those questions welled up inside me with such force I could barely contain myself.

"I think you're onto something," Alexa said, nodding her head. "I'm sure you'll follow through on it."

Running through my mind at that moment was the great conversation Grace and I had earlier that morning. She described how she had changed the questions she was asking about Jennifer, that young woman who works for her. Grace started by asking herself, *What do I want?* and *What are my choices?* She realized all she really wanted was for Jennifer to exercise better judgment and take some initiative. Then she asked what she needed to understand about Jennifer and realized maybe this employee was just afraid of acting on her own.

So there it was, the question that changed everything for Grace in her relationship with Jennifer. It was, *How can I understand?* I thought about that question. It made me wonder how anyone could understand anyone else without considering things from their point of view. That must be what people mean by "walking a mile in someone's moccasins." I began to feel curious about Charles and for the first time really did want to understand where he was coming from.

I remembered my old question I'd reported to Joseph so proudly, *How can I prove I'm right?* Now I saw how that old question had contributed to the team's probably thinking of me as a know-it-all. By changing my question from *How can I prove I'm right?* to *How can I understand?* I began to see Charles in a whole new way. I could hardly wait to get back to my office so I could jot down these insights in my binder.

As Alexa ushered me to the door after our meeting, she commented: "From what I'm seeing, you and Joseph are getting along famously, and you're making wonderful progress."

"Then you think there's some hope for me?" I quipped.

"Oh, I sure do!"

I couldn't wait to get back to my office. With those three simple questions from Joseph's *Top Twelve Questions for Change*, I'd discovered a totally different way of looking at Charles and my conflicts with him. If three of those questions could make that much difference, I wondered what surprises the others held in store for me.

Ben's Breakthrough

I had barely twenty minutes to prepare for my appointment with Charles. I took the time to sit down, catch my breath, and focus my attention on the three questions Joseph had given me for the meeting: *What assumptions am I making? How else might I think about this situation?* and *What is the other person thinking, feeling, needing, and wanting?*

My secretary buzzed, announcing that Charles had arrived. In the past, I would have kept him waiting. Today, I immediately got up and met him at the door. We shook hands, and I asked him how he was doing. He replied that he was okay but a little nervous about this meeting. At least I wasn't the only one. I'd set up our appointment before my meetings with Joseph. At that time, I was ready for a show-down with Charles, and I'm sure he had an inkling of that. Since then, of course, my perspective on the problems between us had changed considerably. I offered Charles a comfortable chair and asked if he'd like coffee or anything to drink. That must have surprised him because I'd never done that in any of our past meetings. He said he was fine, holding up a small bottle of water he'd brought along.

While preparing for this meeting, I recalled that Joseph made sure there was never anything in the space between us. This had the effect of putting me at ease so I fig-ured it couldn't hurt to try the same thing with Charles. I might as well take every opportunity to make this a success-ful conversation. I slid my desk chair over so that Charles and I were sitting near each other by the window. He looked a bit apprehensive at first but seemed to become more comfortable as our meeting moved along.

"I need to hash some things out with you," I began. "And I'd like to start with a few questions."

Charles stared back at me with a slightly worried expression.

"Let me be quite candid with you," I continued. "It's been pointed out to me that my management style has contributed to some of the problems we're encountering with our team. I want to change that, and I believe the place to begin is with our working relationship—yours and mine."

I paused, checking out Charles's reaction. As far as I could tell, he was attentive and engaged. So I continued, "From the start I made some judgments about you based on incomplete information. For example, I knew you'd been here for several years and that you were in line for the job that was given to me. I'm pretty sure my arrival wasn't exactly good news for you, and I assumed you'd have trouble working under me."

Charles nodded. "I've got to confess that's been difficult. Alexa broke it to me gently enough, but that only goes so far."

"I appreciate your honesty," I said. "Had the situation been reversed, I'd have been pretty bent out of shape."

"I'm still working it out," Charles admitted. "Can I ask you this—how am I doing?"

His response surprised me. He'd actually recognized the problem and had apparently been working on it. I had to give him credit for that. "I think you're doing great. What I've been seeing the past few days is that I've got to take responsibility for most of the problems we've been experiencing here. I'm afraid I put an awful lot off on you that really didn't belong in your corner."

"I'm not sure I understand," Charles said.

It wasn't easy saying what I did after that: "I made

two assumptions about you, Charles. First, I assumed that because I was brought in over you that you'd do anything you could to undermine my authority."

"I already admitted that I had trouble being passed over," Charles said, defensively.

"I'm acknowledging that," I told him, feeling a little awkward. "I mention this only to say that I understand now that I have been judging you unfairly." This wasn't easy for me to say. I took a deep breath before going on. "My second assumption had to do with all those questions you ask in meetings."

"Questions? Why are my questions a problem?"

"Let me ask you this, as a reality check. Why do you ask so many questions?"

Charles looked totally bewildered, then gathered his thoughts enough to say, "You're the new guy. I need to find out what you want, what you need, where you're going to take us. How else would I find out things I don't know if I don't ask?"

"There's no problem with that," I said. "The problem has been with me. I've been assuming that you were challenging my authority with all your questions."

"I don't get it."

"Understand this," I said. "I've just come from a job where I was valued for being the guy who always brought answers to the table. I took pride in being called the Answer

Man. But now we're dealing with a very different set of circumstances. I need others to help me find answers."

Charles took a sip of water before he replied.

"There's this guy Alexa brought in for a training session just before you came aboard," he said. "He talked about the powerful impact of questions, how they can help us change our relationships, and even an entire organization. Of everything he taught that day, one thing stands out in my memory. He said, 'Great results begin with great questions.'"

I was stopped cold for a moment. I remembered Alexa telling me about that training the day she hired me. She explained how she was having Joseph come in to facilitate a core training on QuestionThinking. That had been the first reference she ever made to Joseph, and since I hadn't met him yet it hadn't meant much to me. Charles was talking about Joseph, there was no doubt in my mind.

Charles gave me a thumbnail sketch of the training that Joseph had conducted that day. He said he came away with a new respect for how questions can change our thinking and our actions—and, by extension, our relationships and results. I told him I knew Joseph but didn't mention that he was my coach.

"Okay," I said. "I'd like to ask you a question."

"Sure."

"How do we get past what's been blocking us and our

team? You know how urgent it is for us to make changes. In particular, what do you need from me?"

For a moment, Charles seemed taken aback. "I'll have to think about that. But I can tell you this—I'm much more comfortable with you right now than I ever have been before."

"So something I was doing wasn't . . . well, wasn't exactly working for you. Can you help me understand what that was?"

Charles nodded. "I'm not sure I have a simple answer," he told me. "But what I am sure of is that whatever we're doing in this conversation is working a lot better. It seems like a good direction."

"So let's see what we can do to keep up that momentum."

Charles looked thoughtful. "May I make a suggestion? I don't want to overstep my bounds here, but I think I've got something that could be helpful."

My hackles went up. *Here he goes again,* I thought. He's going to challenge my authority. But I stopped myself quickly. In an instant three Self-Q's popped into my mind: *Am I in Judger? How else can I think about this? What do I want to accomplish in this meeting?* I knew I wanted to clear the air with Charles and get the team moving forward. Everything depended on it. Obviously, it was time to let go of some old assumptions.

"I'm all ears," I said. Even as those words left my mouth I felt better.

"It's something Joseph showed us," Charles said. "It's like brainstorming, except with questions."

Just a day before I would have done anything in my power to shut Charles down and take back my authority. Now it felt okay to attempt to collaborate with him.

"Let's start and see how it goes," I said.

Charles went over to the flip chart that had become a permanent fixture in my office and picked up a blue felt-tip marker. "The goal," he explained, "is not to come up with answers, ideas, or suggestions but to come up with as many new questions as possible. Just throw out questions as fast as we can, while I write them down."

"In other words, with no answers or discussions in between," I wanted to make sure I understood.

"Exactly. Joseph said the goal is to open new doors in our minds . . . like behind every door we might find another answer or solution. Every question just expands our range of possibilities. I think his exact words were, 'A question not asked is a door not opened.'"

> # A question not asked is a door not opened.

"That sounds like him," I said. "So where do we begin?"

"You always start by describing the problematic situation and your goals for change. Once you've got those clarified you start the brainstorming process."

"How about focusing on our problems with the team, with the goal of getting us all working together so we can meet our target dates?" I offered.

"Okay," Charles said, writing what I'd said on the flip chart. After that, he immediately added a question that got us rolling: "What do I want to change about the team?"

"What don't we want to change!" I exclaimed. "If we don't get our act together, and soon, it's really going to undermine our getting that new product to market."

"I agree," Charles said. "Let's get that down as a question. Joseph says the best way to do that is to write the questions in the first person. That's what makes this a QuestionThinking exercise."

"Okay," I said, rephrasing my statement: "What would I like to see happen that isn't happening now? What can I do to help us all listen better to each other? What can I do to be more creative? How can I help build a truly collaborative group? What can I do to pull us together . . . like a well-oiled athletic team or maybe a great band?"

"Great questions," Charles said, writing as fast as he could.

I'm not sure where it came from, but right after he

said this, a new question popped out of my mouth: "How can I keep the communication channels open between you and me?"

I thought I saw Charles smile, but he didn't say anything, just wrote my last question on the flip chart. Then he added another of his own: "How can I keep asking Learner questions?"

"How do we state our goals better, so everybody can be more aligned?"

". . . and inspired?" Charles added.

"Exactly," I said.

"Let's keep going. More questions!" Charles exclaimed. He continued to jot down our questions on the flip chart, scrawling out notes with the blue felt-tip pen. For a moment I took myself into observer mode and watched this whole process between Charles and me. I was amazed at how easy and simple it all seemed. I was also amazed at the sheer number of questions. Most remarkable was how naturally Charles and I were working together—like we'd always worked together like this!

"What kind of fuel can I bring to keep our team running?"

"How do I stay out of Judger?"

"How do I define responsibilities for each team member?"

"How do I make sure I follow through on all my promises?"

"How can I assure each member it's really okay to take risks and ask for help?"

We both fired off questions in rapid succession. In no time there were sheets of paper all over the floor. Finally, I suggested we stop and review what we'd done. Charles stepped back from the flip chart and said, "Joseph said it was important, as our first step, to ask if there are any questions on the list we hadn't asked before?"

"Yes, quite a few," I admitted, frankly startled at how many I really hadn't thought about.

Charles and I stood in front of the flip chart and then taped the other sheets up on the wall. We spent the next half hour looking over all our questions and adding new ones here and there. We looked at some of the themes of the questions and prioritized the ones that seemed most important to address first. As we began discussing them, a number of things happened. I got clearer about how we had gotten stuck as well as what we needed to change.

For a moment, I felt apprehensive. Once again, I remembered the first question I'd come up with in Joseph's office only days before: *How can I prove I'm right?* Facing Charles now, I suddenly realized the full consequences that mindset must have had on everyone around me. Frankly, I was embarrassed. It wasn't easy to admit, but it looked as if my old question and my Judger tendencies had been largely responsible for impeding progress for all of us. My Judger questions had discouraged everyone from trying to make a contribution. I'd been miles from the kind of Learner environment that Alexa was so good at creating.

I noticed that seeing all those questions written down like that helped me look at my present situation with the objective eyes of an observer. Almost immediately, I remembered Alexa's story about her big breakthrough, how changing the kinds of questions she asked had changed the whole company. I was getting an inkling of how that could happen for us as well.

Charles was copying our questions into a notebook for later reference.

I perched on the edge of my desk, staring at the flip chart. "I think I have a question to add to our list," I said. I went up to the chart, flipped to a new sheet and wrote, "How can we all make a contribution?"

"Nice," Charles said, nodding.

That word, *contribution*, suddenly became the central focus of my attention. In my zeal to prove I was right, to assert my old role as the Answer Man, I had never asked the questions, *What do I need to understand about this situation? What do other people need? What is my effect on others?* By not asking these simple questions, I'd blocked everyone else from fully participating. I hadn't been open to their contributions at all.

I was staggered by this realization. If only one person could be right—me—then everybody else had to be wrong. What a brilliant way to collaborate! Only one star.

123

It was my fault that the team was failing! I was the problem. My head was spinning. As if that realization about the team wasn't enough, I wondered if my cluelessness had also been the cause of the friction between Grace and me.

A point Joseph made in our first meeting forced its way back into my consciousness. He had said that my question—*How can I prove I'm right?*—would affect *all* my relationships, at home as well as at work. That was hard to take in, but the truth was pretty obvious. Grace had in fact been begging me to open up to her, to let her into my life—so she could give me something. I'd been so busy figuring out how to be right that I wasn't able to listen to her. My wife wanted to contribute to me. I had missed the message altogether because I had been asking the wrong questions!

I pushed thoughts of Grace out of my mind, at least for now. For the time being, I had to focus on Charles and the team.

"I think I could spend the next few hours discussing what we've just accomplished here," I said. "But do you know what the two most valuable lessons are in all of this for me?"

Charles shook his head.

"First, I've got to agree with Joseph that questions have a power all their own, more than I ever knew. Second, I've got a whole new perspective on the importance of understanding and appreciating the people around me."

These revelations were opening another very big door for me, with a new question coming into sharp focus: *How can I allow others to contribute to me?*

"Ben," Charles said. "Before this meeting, I wasn't at all sure I would stay on here at QTec. Frankly, working with you had gotten to be like pulling teeth."

"That painful, huh?" I felt my face break into an embarrassed grin, then I just laughed out loud. "I sympathize with you entirely," I said, extending my hand to him. We had made our peace. In the process I experienced the breakthrough I'd been seeking.

I could hardly wait to tell Alexa about my breakthrough. She was going to appreciate how I'd switched from Judger to Learner by changing my questions. Even more, she was going to love the positive impact I fully believed this would make on the team and the whole company.

After Charles left, I went back to the flip chart and started blocking out plans for a meeting with the team the following morning. This time I wanted to have the right questions to create a Learner environment. I sat down at my desk, pulled out the binder Joseph had given me, and began thumbing through it. I didn't want to miss anything he'd said. I leaned back in my chair and stared at the little placard on the wall: "Question everything!" Yes, I thought, Joseph was right. It all seemed so simple now. Right . . . simple . . . like Einstein's theory of relativity!

Amour! Amour!

9

*T*hat night, charged up by all that happened in the meetings with Alexa and Charles, I worked late. In fact, I worked till long after dark, making notes for the meeting the next morning with Charles and the team. I also made a phone call to Alexa to check on Joseph's availability for meeting with us in the coming weeks. Time raced by. When I remembered to check the clock it was two hours past the time I told Grace I'd be home. I considered calling but figured she'd be in bed sound asleep, so I decided not to disturb her. In the car on the way home I noticed it was going on eleven o'clock.

When I walked in the house I found Grace sitting alone in the dimly lit living room in her pajamas, reading by a single lamp beside her chair. The moment I greeted her, I knew something was wrong. She silently set aside her book, walked up to me, took my hand, led me over to the sofa and told me, gently, to sit down. I sat, half expecting her to announce that someone had died—or that she was leaving me.

Until that evening, I'd never known what it really meant to have a heart to heart talk in which old barriers came down and a relationship made a radical shift. Grace and I had had disagreements and fights in the past but most were flare-ups that never went anywhere. This evening, however, would turn out very differently.

Grace leaned forward in her chair, elbows on her knees, gazing into my eyes in a way that made it quite clear that this was going to be a serious talk.

"Ben," she said, "you have *got* to tell me what's going on with you."

Just as I'd done so many times before, my first reflex was to shrug it off. "I worked late. I told your secretary . . . and I considered calling but figured you were asleep."

"It's not about that. You know it isn't." She fixed me with a stare that told me she wasn't going to back off until she got her way.

"There's been a lot of pressure at work . . . deadlines coming up way too fast . . . but I think there was some real progress today. . . ." I knew I was waffling, but to tell the truth I was scared to death.

Grace shook her head slowly, paused, then asked, "What is it you need right now?"

For a moment I was speechless. Wasn't this the very question I'd asked myself about Charles—and that he had asked me? *What does the other person need?* Was she reading my mind, or had she somehow seen Joseph's *Questions for Change?*

"What do I need?" I echoed nervously. "What do I need! You know, at this point I'm not even sure." I wasn't lying. I really didn't know.

"Let me tell you what I've been noticing," Grace began. "Not long after you took this job, our whole relationship changed. You changed. I began to worry it was something about me. Did you suddenly feel that marrying me had been a mistake? Had I done something that offended or hurt you?"

"Grace, no," I assured her quickly. "It isn't anything like that!"

"That's what I realized after studying the Choice Map," she said. "You know what became clear—that you and I have been going down the Judger path together, judging ourselves and each other harshly, being reactive and defensive, looking to find fault whenever the smallest thing went wrong."

I was bursting to tell her about my breakthrough

with Charles, how it had changed so much for me at work, and how I thought it might make a difference for the two of us. But at this moment what Grace had to say was more important. "I think I understand," I said. "Though it's difficult for me to admit it, that has certainly been true of me."

"I'm filled with questions, but until this afternoon they were mostly Judger ones. I was sure that you and I were in real trouble. Then I started looking for things I might do or say to rescue us from the Judger Pit."

"This is really tough to take in," I said, bowing my head, "I guess there's no easy way to say this . . . no other way through it. . . ."

Grace suddenly looked as pale as a ghost. All the color drained out of her face. "Please let this not be what I'm thinking," she said, her voice shaky and fearful.

I wasn't sure what to say at that moment. All sorts of possibilities were racing through my mind, as I was sure was the case for Grace. She leaned back and huddled in her chair staring at me.

"Wait. What *are* you thinking?" I asked. "Did you think I was going to tell you I was having an affair or something?"

"Well?"

This was an extremely difficult moment for me, for both of us. How could she believe this of me? Did she really think I'd be disloyal to her? How had she come up with that assumption! What could I have done to make her believe that?

"First of all," I began, "I am not having an affair. I would never do that, Grace. But there is something I have to say that is going to be almost as difficult, at least for me."

Grace leaned forward, and I could tell she was a little relieved—but just a little.

"Look, what I'm going to tell you . . . well, I hope you won't end up hating me for it, maybe even as much as if there'd been another woman."

"Just tell me what it is," Grace said. "If we're going to make our relationship work, we've got to be honest with each other. Having the courage to share our fears is part of that, even if it means telling me the worst."

She stopped and stared at me. I guess I was getting a bit emotional at that moment. My eyes were watering up. I could feel my face getting red. I wasn't sure I could say what I knew I had to. I asked myself a thousand questions in that moment, unable to focus on any single one of them. My biggest fear was that Grace would walk out on me when I told her the truth about my problems at work. Would she leave me, just as Jacqueline, my first wife had done years ago? Just before I met Alexa, and she took me on at AZ Corp, I'd lost my job and my wife—all within hours of one another. And believe me, I was certain there was a 50-50 chance I was facing the same crisis again.

"I didn't exactly tell you the truth about Joseph," I began. "As I saw it, I had a choice between going to him for executive coaching or handing in my resignation."

"Your resignation! Oh, Ben, I'm so sorry! Is that what this is all about?"

"For months now I was afraid I wasn't cut out for being a leader," I told her. "And if that didn't work out, I didn't know how it would affect you and me."

We were both silent for several moments, then she asked quietly, "When did you first know things weren't working out in the new job?"

"A few weeks into it," I confessed. "At first it was great. Then I was hit with one challenge after another that I just wasn't able to meet, until I felt like I was drowning. . . ."

"I don't understand."

"You're angry, Grace, aren't you? I was afraid of that." I was convinced, at that moment, that I was about to hear exactly what I'd heard from Jacqueline when she learned that I hadn't gotten the promotion we had counted on.

"You bet I'm angry."

"I just knew it was going to turn out like this. Grace, I'm really sorry. But I think things are turning around for me, in fact, I'm quite sure of it. . . ."

"Wait a second," Grace said. "Back up. You knew *what?* What did you think was going to turn out like this?"

"I went through pretty much this same thing with Jacqueline," I said. "I've got to face facts. I didn't live up to her expectations and I'm not living up to yours. You know what happened between her and me."

"Now wait a minute," Grace interrupted. "Let's not go

Change Your Questions, Change Your Life

off the deep end here. I'm Grace, remember? I'm not Jacqueline. I think you're making some assumptions that aren't necessarily true. Let me just ask you this. Which of my expectations do you think you're not living up to?"

"It's not that I can blame you, Grace . . . I . . ."

"Do you know why I'm angry at you? Do you really know?"

"Of course I do. For screwing up at this job."

"No! No! No! That's not it at all!" She practically screamed at me.

"Then for what?" I asked, totally puzzled. Had she found some offense that was even worse, something I didn't even know about yet? I wracked my brain for an explanation.

"I suppose it's a simple thing," Grace said. "However, it's probably the most important thing in my life where you and I are concerned. It's this—that you haven't been honest with me. You didn't tell me what was going on."

"I had every intention of telling you, but only after I got things rolling again. I was pretty sure I could get a new job right away, and things would get better and you wouldn't ever have to know."

"Listen to me carefully. What makes me angry and sad is that I want you to share these things with me, your troubles, your doubts, your victories, all of it. I share mine with you. That's what marriage is all about, isn't it? When I'm having trouble at work, I talk it over with you, don't I?"

"Sure. I guess you do. I never thought about it."

"Do you remember what I asked you when you came in tonight?"

"Yes, you asked me what I needed."

"You haven't yet answered me," she said. "I want you to."

I sat back in my chair, my jaw dropped, and I just stared into Grace's eyes for a long, long time. I don't know how many minutes passed. Maybe it was just seconds, but they're imprinted in my mind forever. *What do you need?*

"I need . . ." I began, "I guess if I'm being totally honest right now, I need to tell you everything that's been happening to me. I need to be able to tell you the truth and not have my worst fears stop me."

I paused to check out Grace's expression before going on. At first I couldn't tell what she might be thinking. But in spite of not knowing that, I had to continue. Suddenly I felt I had to tell her everything.

"I've had to face my own limitations," I began, working up my courage. "I've had to face the fact that I have been making a lot of assumptions—negative ones—about myself as well as other people. And I've spent way too much time in Judger. All of this has caused major problems at work. And the toughest part I've had to face is that . . . well, I don't have the right answers. I've got a huge amount to learn if I'm going to be able to stay with this job. At least I've got some clearer choices now, thanks to Joseph."

At this point, I poured out the whole story of what I'd gone through the past few months, how I'd been scared to death that if I didn't succeed in this new position, Grace would jump to the conclusion that I couldn't make it at QTec. There had been so many days I felt like a loser that I didn't dare admit I was sliding faster and faster into what Joseph called the Judger Pit. When I got to the end of my story, Grace sat down beside me and draped her arms around me.

"I love you very much," she said. "I love you even more because of what you just shared with me. We can work with this, Ben. But promise me you'll never hold out on me again. It isn't fair to me or to you. Promise?"

"It's not going to be easy," I told her. "Habits are hard to break. Besides, in my work I've learned that you don't get ahead by whining."

"You're not whining! There's a huge difference between being a crybaby and talking so we can figure things out. Besides, I'm your wife. Remember? Sharing brings us closer. There's strength in that. Let's always remember we're in this together."

I knew what she was saying. This conversation was taking the breakthrough I'd had at work to a whole new level. Just as I'd unwittingly prevented my co-workers from making a contribution to me, I'd done the same thing with my wife. You might wonder, did I fully understand it all yet? I'm sure I didn't. But what I did see, quite clearly, was that Joseph's methods worked as well at home as they did at the office.

Until then I'd thought Joseph was simply showing me some skills for the workplace, techniques to get the team working together and save my job. What was becoming clearer by the moment was that these were powerful skills, ones that were as effective with loved ones and friends as with co-workers. These were people skills for my whole life.

Then I was struck with a thought that, to be honest, really got to me—the notion that others, not just Grace, might be *willing* to make a contribution to me. I was not alone!

I covered my face with my hands, not wanting to say anything, afraid I'd lose control if I did. I felt Grace's arms around me and then she snuggled into my lap. She pulled my hands away from my face and kissed me gently on the lips. In that instant, I knew something important had changed, not just between Grace and me but in the whole way I looked at the world.

As we headed upstairs that night, our arms were still around each other, making it difficult to walk. We laughed as we stumbled comically toward the first step. I told her we'd never make it to the top entwined like this.

She smiled playfully: "But we could try."

We kissed again and I suddenly got serious: "Can I ask you a question?"

"Any time," Grace said, with a sparkle in her eyes. "Just anytime at all!"

The Inquiring Leader

Sitting behind my desk at QTec this afternoon, I am remembering that day, nearly five years ago, when I drafted my letter of resignation. So much has changed since then! Joseph's QuestionThinking techniques helped me achieve things I never would have imagined possible. Happily, the benefits of that work have made a huge difference in my personal life as well, and I finally have the kind of marriage I always wanted. Were I ever to forget what seeded all these changes, I'd have only to look at the rosewood paperweight whose silver plaque reminds me that *Great results begin with great questions.*

The changes at QTec have also been significant and dramatic. We've shown consistent profitability for over four years now. Along the way we've had to surmount many hurdles and we've enjoyed at least as many turning points. For me, the first big challenge—and change—occurred through my work with Joseph. At first I was pretty resistant to his ideas, as you may recall. Alexa had introduced him to me as the "inquiring coach," a term I thought was ridiculous. I'm sure that from his point of view I was a hard case, resisting him until his ideas finally started penetrating my thick skull.

What occurs to me as I write this is that the first significant change in my attitude toward Joseph's Question-Thinking methods came that day in my car. Stopped in traffic and late for work, I called him in sheer desperation about my problems with Charles. He told me about his *Top Twelve Questions for Change** and started me off with three questions that he thought might be helpful right away. Those questions, which are such perfect examples of Learner questions, are etched in my brain forever: *What assumptions am I making? How else can I think about this? What is the other person thinking, feeling, needing, and wanting?*

Those few questions helped me cross an important threshold. In the meeting with Charles only a few hours

---

*If you wish to review all *Top Twelve Questions for Change,* see page 167 in the Workbook.

later, everything Joseph had been teaching was validated. I firmly planted my foot on the Learner path with Charles, and together, we went forward. Our collaboration proved infectious with the team, pulling us together and paving the way for the success the company enjoys today.

Joseph's work helped me make some big changes in my relationship with Grace as well. It started that day in the kitchen when she looked at the Choice Map I'd posted on the refrigerator. To my surprise, she loved it and even took the darn thing to work with her! But it was the night I came home late from the office that we had our biggest break-through. Our conversation that night dissolved the wedge between us and created a far more intimate bond.

Happily, that bond has grown deeper and stronger through the years. Up until that point I believed I had to hide my troubles from Grace. Instead, I discovered the strength of true partnership, with loving acceptance, gen-uine curiosity, and working toward shared understanding.

Those turning points, each of them catalyzed by new questions, have changed my mind about a lot of things. I learned how much time I used to spend on the Judger path and how Judger mischief prevented me from moving beyond my own blocks. To tell the truth, I practically lived in Judger, which caused me more grief than I ever could have imagined. Now, whenever I feel those twinges signaling that I've slipped into that Judger place, I quickly reach for my Switching ques-tions to take me back to Learner.

Recently, Joseph's wife, Sarah, interviewed Grace and me for a sequel to their first book on inquiring marriages. It was a real honor to be included. However, what meant even more was the new nickname Grace affectionately gave me during the interview—her *inquiring husband!*

But I'm getting way ahead of my story. Let's go back to that time, six weeks after I drafted my resignation, when I got another call from Alexa that at first unnerved me. My secretary buzzed and said that Alexa wanted me to come to her office right away—and to bring that green folder with me—I'd know the one she was talking about. This sounded pretty ominous because the folder she described held my resignation. Since the breakthrough with Charles, and getting things going with the team, I had thought I was out of the woods. Maybe I was wrong.

I dropped what I was doing, grabbed the folder, and started down the hall. I stood nervously before the big double doors of Alexa's office. Just as I raised my hand to knock, I heard voices inside and wondered what was going on. Rattled by memories of that earlier visit, when I'd first come with resignation in hand, my Judger started clamoring for attention. Instead of responding to it, however, I steadied myself, took a deep breath, stepped into Learner, and knocked lightly on the door.

Seconds later, Alexa was ushering me in. I was surprised to see Joseph waiting in the inner office. He stood up from the sofa and stepped forward a few steps to shake hands with me. As we sat down, I realized that both he and Alexa were in high spirits and seemed happy to see me.

As we made ourselves comfortable, I noticed something in a frame turned face down on the wide coffee table between us. Before I had a chance to ask about it, Alexa pointed to the folder I was holding in my lap and said, "Did you bring the envelope?"

"Envelope?" I asked. My secretary hadn't mentioned anything about an envelope.

"Don't you remember?" Alexa said. "I gave you an envelope with a prediction inside. You put it in that green folder."

I opened the folder immediately. Inside was the envelope she was talking about. Now I remembered. I picked it up and started to hand it to her.

"You open it," Alexa said, "and read it to us."

I tore open the envelope. The note inside, hastily written in Alexa's hand, was very clear: "Ben—in J's Hall of Fame." As I read these words aloud, my voice reflected my puzzlement.

I looked from Alexa to Joseph, searching for some clue about what was going on. Then Joseph picked up the frame I'd noticed and handed it to me. As I turned it over to see what it held, I saw my photo at the top.

"After that meeting between you and Charles," Joseph explained, "I knew you had made the leap over your biggest hurdle. It would only be a matter of time before your results would qualify you for my *QuestionThinking Hall of Fame.*"

I read what he had written, which noted the main question I'd asked before Joseph's coaching and the new question I developed—from *How can I prove I'm right?* to *How can I understand?* As simple as that might look on paper, it was anything but simple in real life. So much had opened up in my life after I began asking *How can I understand?* For example, only then did I become aware of the question, *How can I allow others to contribute to me?* The world I saw after these changes was nothing like what I'd seen before. I really had begun to see with new eyes and hear with new ears. As Joseph once remarked, *Words create worlds.* It was certainly true for me.

Joseph grinned from ear to ear as I took the time to scan what he'd written, outlining why he'd given me this acknowledgment. It also described the breakthroughs that were beginning with my team as a result of adopting QuestionThinking techniques.

It was difficult to imagine myself in Joseph's *Hall of Fame,* but I was deeply touched by the honor. I had to admit that Charles and the rest of our folks had mentioned how much I'd changed. I could hardly deny that kind of proof.

In the weeks following this milestone meeting, I began to notice marked changes in my relationships with just about everyone. Co-workers gave feedback about how much easier it was to be around me. Seeking to understand others and noticing how much they contributed when I gave them half a chance were brand new experiences for me. These changes completely altered how I felt about myself and my job. I couldn't wait to get to work in the morning.

The changes I experienced seemed to ripple through our whole department. Hardly a day went by that I didn't find myself expressing my appreciation for something someone had done. We began to accomplish great things together. Everybody was enjoying the spirit of collaboration. We stopped being a bunch of individuals working separately and, for the first time, truly became a high-performing team.

It was interesting to experience how my new question—*How can I understand?*—allowed me to experience the contributions of others. Within a short time, that question took on a life of its own, allowing other questions to evolve in the same vein, such as *How can I contribute to others?* This additional question added a whole new dimension to my work. I saw that by asking this question, I automatically paid more attention to what others needed and wanted. Everything went easier. Miscommunications were reduced significantly. People shared their ideas, asked lots more questions, and really listened to each other. Truly, these questions were encouraging a level of collaboration and cooperation I'd never even dreamed could exist.

Now let's jump forward another two years in my

story. By then QTec had established a solid and consistent upward trajectory. Our success was noted throughout the business community and was ultimately the subject of a feature article in the *Wall Street Journal*, which attributed our success to "the climate of inquiring leadership that characterizes QTec," as one reporter put it. The day that article came out, Alexa called me to her office. She read me the entire article, emphasizing two places where my name was mentioned. This was just a few hours before she was to leave for a leadership conference in Washington, D.C., where she was giving a presentation she called, *The Inquiring Leader*.

"I'm getting ready to make some major changes at QTec," she said. "There are two things I want to let you know. First, I'm moving Charles into your position. I think he's ready."

For an instant I found myself veering toward the Judger path. The suggestion that Charles would replace me brought up some of my old feelings about him. My Judger reaction startled me, then it quickly faded. In the very next breath Alexa added, "I'd like you to coach Charles through the transition. Then I'm moving you into a new leadership position. I've got big plans for you, Ben, but the details will have to wait until I get back from Washington."

Alexa asked me to tell Charles about his promotion and start building this transition right away. Since we'd worked closely for a couple years, I was certain the changeover would go smoothly.

Things moved along swiftly after that. As soon as Alexa returned from Washington, she scheduled a meeting with Joseph and me. We talked about the progress of the company and the fundamental changes that Question Thinking tools had made possible for QTec.

"The conference in Washington made one thing very clear," Alexa announced. "There's a major change under way in companies like ours. Joseph's ideas are catching on. There's a definite trend toward embracing the principles of *inquiring leadership*. Ben," she paused and smiled, "that reinforces what I'd already decided before my trip to D.C.— to move you into the position of Vice President of Leadership Development."

"That's great news," I said, hardly able to contain my excitement. At the same time I was aware of that old fear in the pit of my stomach. "But I hardly think I'm the one to do that. I'm probably the person who resisted Joseph's teachings the most. This didn't come easily for me, as you know."

Joseph smiled. "That's what makes you the perfect person for the job," he said. "As I told Alexa last week, she needs someone who knows all the arguments for not adopting QuestionThinking. She needs a person who knows what it is to resist with all his might . . ."

"And have his life changed by it," I added easily.

"Any questions?" Alexa asked, turning to me.

"Questions?" I said. "Oh, you bet, millions of them! I've adopted that quote you like so much: *Question everything!*"

Joseph burst out laughing. "You and Alexa make one amazing pair. There are great things happening around here! You're no longer just overcoming limitations. You're creating a new future."

I thought about what Joseph said and recognized how true it was for me . . . and for all of us. In fact, his words propelled my thoughts forward, causing me to wonder, *What other possibilities are about to unfold?*

> **Great results begin
> with great questions.**

QuestionThinking™ *Workbook*

Y ou may recall that at the end of Chapter 3 Joseph gave Ben a binder he called the Question-Thinking Workbook. It contained the seven tools that he introduced to Ben as parts of the QuestionThinking system. The tools in this Workbook appear in basically the same order as in the story. As you go through them, you might want to refer back to how Ben applied and benefited from each one. I've included page references to help you find each tool easily in the story.

Each tool is a facet of the QuestionThinking system and for that reason you may notice they overlap and complement one another. You can use them in business settings as Ben does, by applying them to areas such as team development and leadership development. You can also use these tools to boost your self-confidence, improve your health and well-being, and strengthen all your personal and professional relationships. In my own life, I have yet to find a place where QuestionThinking hasn't made a major contribution, either by itself or as an added value with other systems or ways of working.

There are two key ways to use this workbook:

- Apply the tools to a specific personal or professional situation where you desire a change. Read through the entire workbook and apply each tool to that situation.

- Use the workbook as a reference and reminder of each tool. Quickly skim the material to become familiar with what's offered. You may find your attention drawn to one or more of the tools. Maybe you're reminded that when you were reading Ben's story you thought you'd like to learn more about how to use a particular tool. Or maybe something in his story simply piqued your curiosity.

Whichever way you go, I urge you to actually engage in some of the practices. I notice that when I'm a passenger in a car, I rarely get the directions right. It takes being in the driver's seat, *doing* the driving, to end up where I want to go! Trust yourself. As you look over these pages, let your interest be your guide. Remember, these tools are universal and applicable in an infinite number of ways.

Share this material with others. Feel free to copy any of these QT Tools to show to friends, family, and colleagues. Post any of the tools on your refrigerator and let them stimulate conversation with family members. Put them up at work or bring copies with you to a group or team meeting where QuestionThinking might make a difference.

I'd love to hear from you. I am particularly interested in stories about how QuestionThinking has made a difference in your life—at work and at home.

Workbook Contents

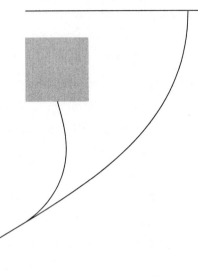

1: Putting The Power of Questions to Work

This tool has two parts: The first has to do with becoming more prolific, intentional, and effective at asking *Internal Questions,* the second has to do with becoming more prolific, intentional, and effective at asking *Interpersonal Questions.*

A: Internal Questions

Purpose: To become more aware of your Self-Q's and to increase the quantity and quality of your internal questions.

Discussion: You may remember that Ben started to change once he realized that, whether he was aware of it or not, questions play a big part in his life. Only following that realization was he able to start refining his questions to take advantage of the tools in the QuestionThinking system. The two practices I present for increasing your awareness of Self-Q's are extremely simple. The first turns your attention to how prevalent internal questions are in your life. The second turns your attention to the types of questions you ask and the kinds of results they produce.

Practice 1: Everything we do in life, all our behaviors, are responses to our internal questions. Even how we go about an everyday activity like getting to work in the morning is based on the questions we ask. Should I drive? Walk? Take a bicycle? Carpool? If I drive, should I take the highway?

Should I take the scenic route? Was there construction on Elm Street? What's going to be fastest? What's going to be safest? What's going to be most enjoyable? The answers to these questions represent the decisions we make. And the decisions we make lead to the results that we get.

When you get up tomorrow morning, do a little research. Take note of the questions you're asking yourself as you decide how you're going to get to work. Then, from time to time throughout the day, ask yourself what questions might be driving your behavior, both your own actions and your interactions with others. It may take some patient probing to recognize these behavior-generating questions, but stay with it until you're able to recognize the influential role Self-Q's play in your life.

Practice 2: As a second piece of research, notice your responses to situations that come up throughout the day. Is your first thought a statement (it may be an opinion or an assumption), or is your first thought a question? If your first thought is a statement, experiment with changing it into a question and notice how that shifts your mood, actions, interactions, or results. What kinds of questions produce what kinds of results?

B: Interpersonal Questions

Purpose: To become more aware of questions you ask others and to increase the quantity and quality of them.

Discussion: The questions we ask others come from the ones we ask ourselves. Some of the reasons for asking questions of other people are to:

- Gather information
- Create understanding and learning
- Build, improve, and sustain relationships
- Clarify and confirm listening
- Stimulate creativity and innovation
- Resolve conflicts
- Create collaboration
- Open possibilities

Imagine trying to do these things without asking questions. The goal is to respond to people and situations with questions and curiosity more often than with answers or opinions.

Practice 1: What is the ratio of questions you ask versus statements you make? During the day, keep a mental scorecard. Does your communication with others involve 80 percent questions and 20 percent statements or answers? Or is it the other way around? What's your typical ratio? In at least one conversation today, practice asking 80 percent questions.

Practice 2: Recall a time when you encountered a question that made a positive difference in your life. It might be a question you asked someone else or one that someone asked you. It might have been in a personal or professional situation. What was the question? What was the result? What was it about the question that made such a difference?

Practice 3: Notice times during the day when you want to ask someone a question but are reluctant to do so. Get curious about what might be in the way. Then wonder about what it would take to get the courage to ask. Observe what happens when you do ask questions as well as what happens when you don't.

2: Choice Map

(See pages 32–33 for full graphic.)

Purpose: To use the Choice Map as a visual summary of the Learner-Judger mindsets and the futures that they can lead to.

Discussion: Throughout Ben's story, the Choice Map is a core guide that helps him become aware of the questions he's asking, how they affect his actions, and how they influence his results. The map allows Ben to locate where he's operating at any moment and consider how he might change his questions for different results. Here are four ways this tool can be applied:

Practice 1: Imagine you're standing at the crossroads of the Choice Map, considering what to do about a situation in your business or your career. Or it might be in your personal life, with your family, friends, health, or personal development. Experiment by asking yourself both Judger and Learner questions about this situation. Notice how each kind of question affects you, and where each takes you on the map. If you land in Judger, consider what Switching question might allow you to step onto the Switching Lane and back up to Learner territory. Looking at the Choice Map, you can simply ask: *Where am I right now? Am I in Judger? Where do I want to be? What questions would help me get there?*

Practice 2: You can use the Choice Map to learn from a past situation that didn't work out as you would have liked. The Choice Map can help you discover if any Judger mischief blocked your success. If so, what lessons can you learn from this? How would you handle that same situation now with the knowledge and skills gained from this book?

Practice 3: You can also use the Choice Map to learn from a situation that *did* work to your satisfaction. What Learner questions made the difference for you? How did those questions help you avoid the Judger Pit? If any Judger was present, which Switching questions did you use to move onto the Learner path? What lessons can you draw from these observations that you might want to reinforce and benefit from again in the future?

Practice 4: Explain the Choice Map to someone else and you'll gain at least as much as you give. There's an old medical school saying: "See one, do one, teach one, and it's yours!" This is an ideal way to reinforce Learner partnerships with the people around you.

3: Learner-Judger Questions

(See page 49 for the graphic of Learner-Judger Questions and page 78 for the full Learner-Judger Chart.)

Purpose: To use these charts to help distinguish between our Learner and Judger mindsets and how they affect our thinking, actions, relationships, and results.

Discussion: In the story, Joseph shows Ben how to use the chart of Learner-Judger Questions to identify the kinds of questions he's asking and notice their impact on himself, other people, and situations around him. The following exercise allows you to have an experience similar to Ben's:

Practice: Look at the Learner-Judger Questions and slowly read all the questions in the Judger column, either silently or out loud. Notice how the questions affect you physically and emotionally. If you're like most people, Judger questions may lead you to feel de-energized, fearful, negative, tense, or even a little depressed. When I do this exercise in workshops, people report holding their breath, feeling suddenly stressed, or even getting a headache. They're often amazed by how quickly this experience impacts them.

Now it's time for Learner. Take a deep breath, let go of Judger, and slowly read the Learner questions on the right side of the chart. Notice how you feel now. People often report that Learner questions can make them feel energized, optimistic, open, hopeful, and relaxed. They feel encouraged to look for solutions and possibilities. As one man noted, "When I'm looking with Learner eyes, I feel hopeful about the future."

As you went over these lists and noticed your different responses, you may have discovered, as Ben did, how questions associated with these different mindsets can put you in distinctly different moods. As you become familiar with these contrasting mindsets, also explore how one or the other impacts how you feel about relating to people around you. Ask yourself how Judger mindset—yours or theirs—might affect communications with a co-worker, spouse, child, or friend. Then ask the same question about how Learner mindset impacts communications, experiences, and results.

4: Empowering Your Observer Self

(Review pages 68–69 for a reminder of how the observer self applies to choosing and switching from Judger to Learner.)

Purpose: To awaken or strengthen the observer part of ourselves so we can note our own thoughts, feelings, and actions more objectively.

Discussion: In Chapter 3, Ben learns how to make use of that part of himself called the observer. As Joseph points out, we all have this observer capacity. It is simply the ability to stand outside ourselves and witness what we are thinking, feeling, or doing. You may have experienced this for yourself—feeling as if you were watching a movie and you were an actor in it.

Is it ever possible to become 100 percent objective and open? Probably not. But to be able to switch into observer mode to any degree can be an invaluable asset for self-understanding, negotiating change, making decisions, operating effectively under pressure, and relating well to others. This observer capacity also builds the kind of awareness that is the cornerstone of emotional intelligence. From observer we are in an ideal position to recognize what kinds of questions we're asking, and to switch to Learner when we find ourselves on the Judger path.

Building our observer allows us to develop a calm center of equanimity. We become somewhat detached from our own thoughts and feelings. Being right or wrong is less important and we are less attached to outcomes. Many spiritual and philosophical traditions have this observer capacity at their core. It is also a natural ability that is strengthened by meditation.

Condition your observer "muscles" through regular practice, even if it's just for a few minutes a day. The goal is to develop the ability to be still, calm, and present with ourselves and others. Then, when you need the solid foundation the observer self offers, it is already there for you. Many fine books offer awareness training and meditation instruction, which you can find in most bookstores and libraries.

Here are two simple ways to start empowering your observer capacity right now:

Practice 1: The next time your phone rings, at home or at work, be still and just let it ring. In fact, listen to the ringing. As you do, notice your desire to act—to rush to the phone and pick it up—or your desire to avoid it. Carefully observe what is going through your mind and body, without taking action (i.e., answering the phone) or becoming attached to the thoughts and feelings that were triggered by the ringing phone.

If you wish, imagine that your thoughts and feelings are like clouds moving across the sky and you're simply watching the shifting picture.

When you get into a challenging situation and you have an impulse to act, or have thoughts or feelings you want to express, step into observer mode instead. Remind yourself that, just as with the ringing phone, you do not have to "answer" those impulses. You can learn to simply watch. Then, when you do take action, it will be more thoughtful, strategic, and mindful of potential consequences.

Practice 2: The next time you're faced with an important choice, or when you have slipped into your Judger-head, take a few quiet minutes to be alone. Sit quietly, noting whatever you are thinking, feeling, or wanting at that moment. Promise yourself that regardless of what you observe, this is not yet a time for action. Simply observe and note.

In the most expansive sense, the observer is calmly asking a single Self-Q: *What's present now?* . . . moment by moment by moment. As your observer becomes more robust and effective, you will become ever better at recognizing when you're in Judger. It is this moment of "wake-up," noting where you are, that grants you the power of true choice.

5:   Switching Questions

(Read pages 69–70 for a reminder of what Joseph taught Ben about Switching questions.)

Purpose: To learn to use Switching questions to make a course correction from the Judger path onto the Learner path and Learner possibilities.

Discussion: A Switching question is a special kind of Learner question. As you'll recall from Ben's story, he learns to ask Switching questions whenever he finds himself in Judger. Keep the Choice Map in mind. It'll help you remember to use this shortcut from Judger back to Learner.

Think of Switching questions as "rescue questions," "turnaround questions," or "course correction questions." They can literally *rescue* you from Judger experiences or consequences once you've recognized that's where you are. Switching questions give you the opportunity to choose a new direction, and sometimes make major breakthroughs—both with yourself and in your relationships with others.

By their very nature, Switching questions are "to-from" questions, meaning they can carry you to a Learner mindset whenever you notice you're in Judger. Whether or not you realize it, you already have Switching questions of your own. The best ones are those that feel most natural and accessible to you. These are the questions you most easily and consistently reach for and use. The more "grooved in" they are, the more effective they can become. The following list of random questions includes some contributed by participants in workshops over the years.

- Am I in Judger?
- Where would I rather be?
- How can I get there?
- What are the facts?
- How else can I think about this?
- What assumptions am I making?
- Is this what I want to feel?
- Is this what I want to be doing?

- What am I missing or avoiding?
- How can I be more objective and honest?
- What is the other person thinking, feeling, needing, and wanting?
- What humor can I find in this situation?
- What's my choice right now?

This is an evolving, growing list. Add your own questions as you think of them.

Practice 1: Think of a past situation that was difficult or frustrating for you but which you managed to turn around. It's likely that you used Switching questions to do it but didn't recognize them at the time. Think about what your Switching questions might have been. Why do you believe they made a difference? When you discover what Self-Q's you asked intuitively, you'll be able to ask them more intentionally, skillfully, and quickly. You can use the above list to jog your memory about what those questions might have been.

Practice 2: Pick a Switching question, either from the list or your own experience, to put into practice for a few days. After that, pick another one. Keep going. Notice the effect on you as well as others when you ask these different questions. Which ones seem familiar, easy, natural, and most helpful? Are some more useful in one kind of situation or relationship than another? Experiment and find out.

Practice 3: The A-B-C-C Choice Process. Pick another challenging situation where you desire a change and follow the format described on pages 84–85 of Ben's story.

6: Questioning Assumptions

Purpose: To avoid making mistakes based on false or incomplete information.

Discussion: Assumptions are invisible chains to the past that block freedom of choice and action for the future. To make an assumption is to presume or believe something to be true without first asking questions to verify if it really is. It's all too easy to overlook assumptions or defend them without question. Until we bring them to light, assumptions can sabotage our efforts to achieve our goals and deepest desires. Once we are able to make these blind spots visible, we gain new insights and creative possibilities that allow us to move forward in more positive and productive ways.

Assumptions also undermine effective communication. Assumptions can make it difficult to build or maintain satisfying relationships. For example, Ben assumes that Charles's persistent questioning is an effort to sabotage him. This assumption prevents Ben from discovering Charles's true motivation—finding out what Ben wants or needs. Remember, also, that Grace makes assumptions about Jennifer, her assistant, which renders her ineffective as a manager until she questions her assumptions and checks with Jennifer to discover what's true for her.

How do you detect your own assumptions so they don't trip you up? First is the willingness to discover them. The habit of asking skillful questions, both of ourselves and others, is our best tool for uncovering blind spots and moving beyond them to discover valuable information, perspectives, and possibilities.

Practice: Think of a personal or professional situation in which you are stuck, frustrated, or want a change. Use the following list of assumption-busting questions to help you take a disciplined approach to unearthing assumptions that might be blocking or limiting your success. For best results, consider each question thoroughly in light of the specific situation and write down what you discover. Often, the very act of writing it out can stimulate deeper reflection and discoveries.

- What assumptions am I making about *myself,* for example, my capabilities and commitments?
- What assumptions am I making about *others,* for example, their capabilities and commitments?
- What am I assuming, based on previous experiences, that may not be true *now?*
- What am I assuming about available resources?

- What limitations am I assuming to be so—and what surprises might I find?
- What am I assuming about external circumstances or "reality"?
- What am I assuming about what's impossible—or about what's possible?

7: The Top Twelve Questions for Change

(See Chapter 7, page 99)

Purpose: To provide a logical sequence of questions for assuring that you cover all the bases before making a change or embarking on a new direction.

Discussion: In Chapter 7 Ben is caught in traffic. He calls Joseph, who gives him three of the *Top Twelve Questions for Change*. Those three questions cause Ben to reassess his relationship with Charles. Later, they help him discover a better way of working with his team. This, in turn, leads to a breakthrough for his company and puts Ben in line for a major promotion. Still later, those same three questions help Ben create a significant turnaround in his relationship with his wife, Grace.

The questions on the *Top Twelve* list evolved out of my work with coaching clients and workshop participants over many years. The list can be used in at least three ways: First, it is a logical sequence of questions to help work through any situation you might want to change or improve. Second, you might just scan the list for questions you've been missing. Third, you can turn to it when you're looking for just the right question to emphasize in a particular situation.

Within this list are questions that are applicable to a variety of life's challenges. The goal is to integrate these questions into your everyday thinking. Then, when a challenge arises, you'll be able to easily recall some of them. Not every question applies to every situation. That's why you'll want to develop a collection of your favorites and work with them on a regular basis. These questions can open and change your mind. They allow you to unveil new choices, options, and possibilities you might otherwise miss.

Practice: As in the Assumptions practice, think of a situation in which you are stuck, frustrated, or want something to change. You can ask each question on the list below from several perspectives. Ask them of yourself—*What do I want?* Ask them of other people—*What do you want?* Or ask these questions of those with whom you have a relationship—*What do we want?*

The Top Twelve Questions for Change

1. What do I want?
2. What are my choices?
3. What assumptions am I making?
4. What am I responsible for?
5. How else can I think about this?
6. What is the other person thinking, feeling, needing, and wanting?
7. What am I missing or avoiding?
8. What can I learn
   . . . from this person or situation?
   . . . from this mistake or failure?
   . . . from this success?
9. What questions should I ask (myself and/or others?)
10. What action steps make the most sense?
11. How can I turn this into a win-win?
12. What is possible?

Keep this list in a handy place where you can refer to it whenever you feel stuck or might wish to seek new alternatives. Of course, you can also add any questions that you discover might be useful for you.

Afterword

While Ben's story is fiction, it is filled with truth. I have seen these same kinds of remarkable results unfold for many of the women and men to whom I've taught these principles, through individual coaching, seminars, and in the organizations where I consult. In a way, it's their stories I've shared with you through Ben. It's also my story. What I told you in the Introduction about using these same skills and tools in my own life is true. I know that without QuestionThinking strategies I could never have written this book. If I didn't work daily at practicing what I preach,

I'm sure I wouldn't co-own several companies or have such a deeply satisfying marriage.

Like many authors, I am motivated by a fervent desire to share with others what I've learned personally. Now that you've read Ben's story and looked over the workbook, I would like to believe that you're already beginning to reap some of the benefits of what you've learned about QuestionThinking. Anwar Sadat said that, "He who cannot change the very fabric of his thought will never be able to change reality." Our internal questions *are* the very fabric of our thinking. This is the basis of my claim that if you change your questions, you really can change your life.

The more we bring Learner thinking and Learner action into our relationships at home and at work, the more positively we can affect ourselves and the people and organizations around us. Imagine what our world would be like if we had inquiring leaders, inquiring teams, inquiring organizations, and inquiring marriages! And what if we brought these same principles to parenting and education? While Judger begets Judger, it's even more powerful to remember that Learner begets Learner.

So here is my final question for you:

What changes do you want to make in your life?

Notes

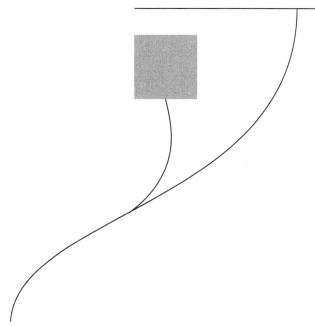

My professional text, *The Art of the Question: A Guide to Short-Term Question-Centered Therapy,* was published by John Wiley & Sons in 1998. My name then was Marilee Goldberg.

Page 68: This quote is from *Man's Search for Meaning: An Introduction to Logotherapy* by Viktor E. Frankl, originally published in Austria in 1946. The English translation was first published by Beacon Press in Boston in 1959, and the latest edition was published in 1984.

Page 89–90: Campbell's story of the farmer and the quote, "Where you stumble, there your treasure is," come from *An Open Life: Joseph Campbell in Conversation with Michael Toms,* edited by Michael Toms and published by Harper & Row in 1988.

Page 142: "Words create worlds," Cooperrider, D., Barrett, F., and Srivastva, S. (1995). "Social Contruction and Appreciative Inquiy: A Journey in Organizational Theory" in (Hosking, D., Dachler, H., and Gergen, K. eds.)

Management and Organization: Relational Alternatives to Individualism, Aldershot UK: Ashgate Publishing Limited.

Page 170: This quote is from Anwar Sadat's *In Search of Identity: An Autobiography,* published in 1978 by Harper & Row.

About the Author

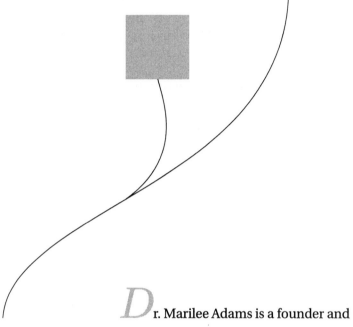

*D*r. Marilee Adams is a founder and partner with the Center for Inquiring Leadership and the originator of QuestionThinking™. As a thought leader, executive coach, and consultant to some of the world's most elite companies, Marilee has witnessed the power of QuestionThinking to transform leaders, strengthen teams, and contribute to building inquiring organizations.

QuestionThinking methods and tools are benefiting employees in Fortune 100 companies and the federal government, from Lockheed Martin, Siemens Building Technologies, and Aetna U.S. HealthCare, to The National

Defense University, and NASA Goddard. As a professional speaker, Marilee's presentations on the art of Question-Thinking and Inquiring Leadership have been applauded by numerous organizations, audiences, and media venues.

In her previous career as a psychotherapist for over twenty-five years, Marilee facilitated individuals, couples, and families in using the spirit of inquiry to create remarkable new possibilities for themselves.

Marilee earned her Ph.D. in Clinical Psychology from the Fielding Institute in Santa Barbara, California, and a Masters in Social Work from Virginia Commonwealth University. She is on the faculty for the Institute for Life Coach Training and a guest lecturer at Columbia University Teacher's College.

Marilee's first book, *The Art of the Question: A Guide to Short-Term Question-Centered Therapy* (John Wiley & Sons, 1998) has been lauded as a "seminal and breakthrough contribution to the field of psychotherapy." Marilee has also published articles on the expert use of questions in coaching, business, and organizational transformation. Most recently, she co-authored, with Marge Schiller, Ph.D. and David Cooperrider, Ph.D., a chapter for the book series, *Advances in Appreciative Inquiry.*

Marilee is impassioned by questions and their power to create new, enlivening possibilities for individuals and organizations. She believes that we build our worlds with our questions, and creating real change and new possibili-

---

About the Author

ties requires asking new ones, both of ourselves and each other. She works very hard to live the principles in this book and hopes that you will also take them to heart and enjoy the benefits.

Marilee and her husband, artist Ed Adams, live in the river town and arts community of Lambertville, New Jersey. She invites your thoughts and questions at Marilee@MarileeAdams.com or through www.CenterforInquiring Leaderhship.com.

About the Center for Inquiring Leadership

The Center for Inquiring Leadership (CIL) is a training and consulting organization dedicated to bringing the benefits of QuestionThinking™ to organizations, teams, and individuals as well as to our relationships at work and in our personal lives. These QuestionThinking methodologies, skills, and tools are at the heart of CIL's work, from leadership and organization development to corporate coaching certification programs.

A core offering of CIL is a workshop entitled *The Inquiring Leader: Coaching and Mentoring for Results*. This workshop provides an opportunity for leaders and managers to develop coaching skills that help inspire the best thinking, innovation, collaboration, and results in their teams and organizations.

Another main offering is a workshop entitled *Coaching for Human Resource Professionals*. This program builds coaching skills that contribute to Human Resource professionals transforming their role from a transactional one to a strategic partnership.

We welcome your inquiries about other workshops as well as our services, products, keynotes, and learning community.

Center for Inquiring Leadership
160 Lawrenceville-Pennington Road, Suite 16, # 116
Lawrenceville, New Jersey 08648
Phone: 609-730-4892 or 800-250-7823
Email: Info@InquiringLeader.com
Web: www.CenterforInquiringLeadership.com